THE AVRO VULCAN
- CELEBRATING 60 GLORIOUS YEARS -

Contents

Written by Mark Freshney, Robert Miller and John Wood
with Ian Homer and Barry Masefield

Compiled and edited by Mark Freshney

First published 2012
ISBN 978-0-9567880-1-6

Written by Mark Freshney, Robert Miller and John Wood
with Ian Homer and Barry Masefield
Compiled and edited by Mark Freshney
Design/artwork by www.underthefloor.co.uk

1st Impression. © Vulcan to the Sky Trust, November 2012
Published by the Vulcan to the Sky Trust
(Registered Charity No. 1101948)
1 & 2 Venture Court, Dodwells Road
Hinckley, Leicestershire LE10 3BT

Printed in the UK by Stephens & George Print Group,
Goat Mill Road, Dowlais, Merthyr Tydfil CF48 3TD

We would like to express our sincere thanks to all the supporters
who share our passion for XH558 and those who have provided
their photographs to help secure her future.
In all cases, copyright is held by the photographer and images
have been reproduced with their kind permission.
Contributor articles remain the copyright of the authors.

For more information on the Vulcan to the Sky project, including flight updates, please visit
www.vulcantothesky.org

A range of official Vulcan to the Sky merchandise is available at
www.vulcantotheskystore.co.uk

Foreword

by Eric Verdon-Roe

Grandson of Sir Alliott Verdon-Roe

The Avro Vulcan is probably the most evocative aircraft ever to have been built. I have marvelled at it on many occasions and have always been impressed by its ability to awe inspire a crowd. It is a great privilege to have a family link with the Vulcan, not only as the grandson of Sir Alliott Verdon-Roe, co-founder of Avro with his brother Humphrey, but also because I share a birthday with the Vulcan in August 1952. I have therefore always thought of the Vulcan as a close family member!

From the humble beginning of his 1909 Triplane, the first all British aeroplane to fly, A.V. Roe created A.V. Roe & Co. in Manchester, that grew into one of the largest companies in Britain just 10 years later. The Vulcan was the latest, loveliest, loudest, and last, in a series of great military designs including the 504, Anson, Lancaster and York. After designing the original 504, A.V. Roe handed design over to his protégé Roy Chadwick who worked on all these aircraft, including laying down the original design of the Vulcan before his tragic death. His designs therefore spanned from biplane to V-Bomber.

The work that has gone into flying and maintaining Vulcan XH558 over the past six years has been truly remarkable and the affection with which it is held by the British public is shown by the many, many thousands who have pledged their support to keep this great aircraft flying. Every one of them should be very proud of what has been achieved.

I look forward to the Vulcan XH558 finding a permanent site where it will be able to continue being displayed and demonstrated in all its glory, so that it can inspire future generations as a great example of the excellence of British engineering and creativity.

Eric Verdon-Roe
Sherborne, Dorset

Exercise 'Mayflight': nine Vulcan bombers from three squadrons lined up at RAF Scampton on 11 May 1961. The flight line consists of XJ782, 783, XH554, 563 (all 83 Squadron), XJ823 (27 Squadron), XH558, 562, 561 & 559 (230 OCU). *Lincolnshire Echo*

Once in a while, a creation of human skill and design and ingenuity makes its mark on everyday life. In aeronautical terms, ask most people and there can be no better examples than iconic aircraft such as the Spitfire, the Lancaster and Concorde.

One other aircraft has rightly earned its place with that illustrious company, being instantly recognisable, and also having endeared itself in the hearts of an enthusiastic public. Like the other aircraft, it was designed for a specific purpose, and pushed the boundaries of what the British aviation industry could achieve at the time. The result: a design that led the world and one that still looks startlingly modern.

So in 1952 was born the Avro Type 698, soon to be called Avro Vulcan, the major part of Britain's strategic deterrent V-force and the mainstay of the RAF strike capability throughout the 1960s and 1970s. That there is one example still flying in 2012 is testament to the team that designed the aircraft type from as early as 1947, and a full 60 years after the prototype first took to the skies.

This book celebrates a wonderful aircraft with an overview of the company behind its design and construction, its people, the developments along the way, its varied service life and the time the Vulcan went to war. This book looks at the Vulcan fleet and records some of the memories of the people who flew and maintained them, whilst also focusing on the remarkable story and survival of the sole remaining airworthy example - Vulcan XH558

the '*Spirit of Great Britain*'.

A.V. Roe

A short history of the founder and company

The early years

Edwin Alliot Verdon Roe was born in April 1877, the son of a doctor from Salford, Manchester. Verdon was his mother's maiden name which he adopted later by deed poll in her honour. Having left home at just 14 for a short lived opportunity in Canada, he settled for a career in the Merchant Navy, where he became aware of the potential of powered flight in the pioneering days of the early century, and perhaps being inspired by the gliding techniques of albatrosses seen on many of his voyages, began to make several small scale models to investigate his own ideas further.

Having entered and won a £75 prize in a Daily Mail competition with one of his model aircraft designs in 1907, he began working at his brother's house in Putney to develop further his Roe I Biplane to full size and to begin flight trials. To achieve this, he set up small workshops, first at Brooklands, then at Walthamstow Marshes, near London, where he made the first all British flight across the marsh in 1909, flying his Roe I Triplane.

Although more a series of short hops, flushed with this initial success and the huge potential before them, Alliott and his younger brother Humphrey, agreed to go into the aircraft business together. Humphrey would provide finance, organisation and management skills as well as factory space at his existing business, Everard and Co. in Ancoats, Manchester. This was a traditional cotton mill, producing garments and products like gentleman's braces. The industry had seen rapid decline since the Cotton famine of the 1860s, so it was a natural fit to have the factory space allocated to other work and indeed, to be able to prepare

Edwin Alliot Verdon Roe, in a portrait by Bassano. *National Portrait Gallery*

Verdon Roe in front of his Roe I Triplane on the tow path of the River Lea by the railway arches (above), and standing by the Roe I at Blackpool Aviation Week. *Verdon-Roe*

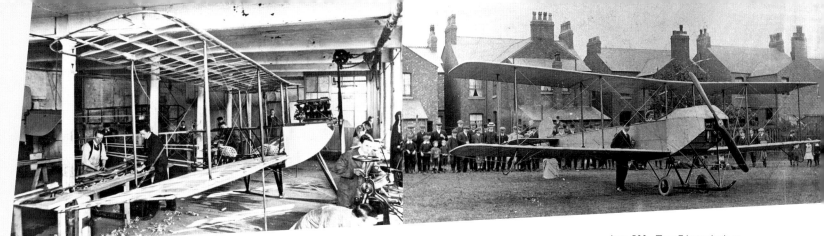

Avro 500 - Type E being built at Brownsfield Mill in 1912, a young Roy Chadwick is thought to be the onlooker to the left of the engine block. *BAE Systems*

sewn by hand cotton coverings to the wings and control surfaces that would cover the early prototypes. Alliott would then be free to concentrate on design and testing.

So, on 1 January 1910, A.V. Roe and Co was formed. This date represents the beginning of the company as a real business and Humphrey rather modestly became the 'and Co' in A.V. Roe and Co.

In Britain in the early 1900s, there were few competitors. The majority of aeroplanes flown at that time were being imported from France, where early pioneers like Blériot were already well established. (Blériot was actually the first man to fly the English Channel in 1909 with one of his own machines - winning a £1,000 prize offered again by the Daily Mail newspaper).

The first aircraft produced by the new company was the Roe II Triplane, one of a series of early designs that culminated in the Avro 500 biplane of 1912. A.V. Roe was responsible for a number of 'firsts', amongst them - the Avro Type F of 1912, the first aircraft to fly with an entirely enclosed cockpit.

All of these early aircraft were produced in very small numbers, but the Avro 504 would change all that, with over 8,000 built over two decades. A tiny number of these aircraft saw front line service during the First World War with the Royal Flying Corps, who subsequently used the aircraft as the basic trainer on the establishment of the Royal Air Force in 1918, when they merged with the Royal Naval Air Service.

This marked the beginning of the aviation business in the North West, which at its peak, employed hundreds of thousands of people in the region. Avro and A.V. Roe & Co were to go on to produce some of the most iconic aeroplanes of the 20th century.

Below left: The Avro F, the first aircraft with an enclosed cockpit. Below: The Avro 504. *Verdon-Roe*

Above: The Avro works at Alexandra Park in 1923, just before the move to Woodford.
Ringwayobserver

Above right: The Shuttleworth Collection's Avro 621 Tutor in 2008. This aircraft was used for communication duties during the Second World War. After suffering engine failure during the filming of Reach for the Sky it was purchased by the Shuttleworth Collection and restored to flying condition. This photo shows it flying in the colours of the Central Flying School, representing airframe K3241.

The inter-war years

During the closing days of World War 1, with the assistance of the War Department, Avro were able to establish their own airfield facilities near to the factory at what was to become known as Alexandra Park Aerodrome. It was ideal for aircraft development and testing of new machines and of course, for pilot training in the war effort. Parts would be taken for assembly from the factory, transported by road and by rail, as the nearby railway station had given the site its name.

However, peacetime brought a drastic reduction in military orders and placed severe financial pressures on Avro, forcing them to release over 68% of the company shares in 1920 to Crossley Motors, a local vehicle body building company who were in desperate need of production facilities. Under their investment, Avro were able to undertake an expansion programme that included moving away from the small grass airfield to an area that could offer scope for further expansion. With the land lease fixed to expire five years after cessation of war, Avro needed to find an alternative site quickly.

In 1924, the Company moved to a rural site further south of the growing city at New Hall Farm, Woodford. By 1928, Crossley's had decided to sell Avro to Armstrong Siddeley which resulted in Alliot resigning from the company he had founded, to begin again with the formation of Saunders-Roe, taking a controlling interest in Isle of Wight boat builders, S.E. Saunders. His interest now was in the design and building of flying-boats, seen as having great potential in carrying heavy loads long distances without the need of restrictive runway locations. The '30s were to see what many call the 'Golden Age' of this mode of transport, before the outbreak of war would change the face of aviation once again.

Back at Woodford, Avro were continuing their long legacy of training aircraft with the development of the Avro Tutor, a steel framed doped linen clad design by Roy Chadwick. This aircraft, first flown in 1930, and its many variants would form a long list of other similar designs from the designer and his team throughout this intense period of development, perhaps with his vision personified by the Avro Anson, a twin engine monoplane of all metal construction that first flew a few years later in 1935.

This held the distinction of being the first aircraft in the RAF to offer a retracting undercarriage, albeit, at first, through a long and demanding hand-cranking mechanism operated by a member of the crew!

In the Avro Anson, perhaps you can see the beginnings of another famous aircraft to come from the same design stable of Roy Chadwick and the Woodford plant just six years later. The aircraft was a good solid base for multi-engine pilot training, a rapid requirement of the many changing designs during that era. Once again, it was work that held Roy and Avro in high esteem for the challenges that were to come as the storm clouds of war gathered over Europe once more.

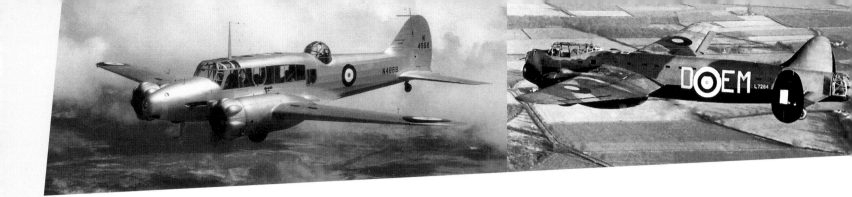

1935 was also a time of great change for Avro as it became part of the Hawker Siddeley Group when Hawker Aircraft orchestrated a series of mergers and acquisitions that not only involved them, but J.D. Siddeley, their own engine division of Armstrong Siddeley, together with Armstrong Whitworth Aircraft and the Gloster Aircraft Company. Many would retain their own identities and projects, but the consolidation would now lead to much closer collaboration on future work.

The Avro 652 Anson and 679 Manchester.

The Second World War period

By 1937, Avro were already looking more to military applications and design work began on a twin-engine bomber to be called The Manchester. After flight trials and various alterations, it soon became apparent that the aircraft suffered from a severe lack of power for carrying heavy loads and development work was taken over to the recently opened Ringway Airport, a little further west of the existing Woodford site to see what structural changes and power-plant options could offer better performance.

As war loomed, this became the base for RAF Ringway and an Avro production satellite was established for the war effort, supplemented by a new plant to the north of Manchester at Chadderton, then at Newton Heath to the east of the city and another at Yeadon, near Leeds. Woodford was deemed to be very susceptible to enemy attack and having the work spread like this gave extra security to the many projects in hand and vital production lines. (Ringway would become better known post-war as Manchester International Airport, while Yeadon is now the site of Leeds Bradford Airport).

By 1941, to meet a more stringent Air Ministry specification, Roy Chadwick and his team had defined the Avro Lancaster, with four engines on a much larger wing. Between them, the Avro sites and various appointed sub-contractors (including Austin Motors at Longbridge in Birmingham) were to go on to produce over 7,300 of the bombers powered by the equally famous Rolls-Royce Merlin engine. At the height of the Second World War, Avro had over 29,000 people working in the Manchester area alone, more than a third of them women, many with no previous manufacturing skills.

The legendary Avro 683 Lancaster, and production in full swing at the Avro factory.

Top sequence:
Lancaster derivatives
the York, Lancastrian,
Lincoln and Shackleton.

Below left to right:
Gathered at Woodford
on 9 September 2012,
Martin Withers DFC,
Geoffrey Falk, younger
son of Roly Falk, the
test pilot on the Vulcan's
maiden flight, Harry
Holmes Chairman
of the Avro Heritage
Centre, ex Vulcan
pilot Geoffrey New,
now restoring an Avro
504, John Falk, elder
son of Roly Falk, Eric
Verdon-Roe, grandson
of Alliott Verdon-Roe
the founder of A.V. Roe
& Co.
*David Fildes - Avro
Heritage Centre*

So successful was the Lancaster design that it would go on to provide the basis for several other Avro aircraft during and immediately after the war, including the Lincoln bomber, Lancastrian airliner, York transport and Shackleton maritime patrol aircraft. The York flew half of the British contribution to the Berlin Airlift, over 58,000 sorties, and the Shackleton served the RAF for nearly 40 years until retired in 1990.

Postwar developments

The Second World War ended following the dropping of two atomic bombs on Japan. With the advent of these new, terrifyingly powerful weapons, military strategy changed significantly, and as a result, the requirements for new aircraft designs. The British, after many consultations with the Americans over shared information and technology, soon realised that an independent atomic weapons capability would be needed and by default, an aircraft capable of carrying a heavy bomb-load long distances.

Avro and Roy Chadwick would need to step up to the challenge again. So was born the Avro 698, later to be called the Avro Vulcan and the subject of this book. By 1963, the company had been fully absorbed into Hawker Siddeley Aviation and the Avro name ceased to be used, only to be recalled for use in a series of small regional jets made by the now renamed British Aerospace as a result of more mergers within the industry. Today, that company is now the massive British multinational defence, security and aerospace company - BAE Systems.

A.V. Roe himself in later years.

After his resignation from Avro, Alliot moved to Hamble in Hampshire to be near his Saunders Roe Flying Boat operations. He was knighted in 1929 for his services to aviation, and had also been honoured with an OBE and Hon.FRAeS. In 1933 Alliot changed his surname to Verdon-Roe by deed poll, adding the hyphen between his

last two names in honour of his mother. He lost two of his sons during the Second World War when they were killed in active service while in the RAF. In later years, his companies, interests and engineering projects included speedboats, jet and rocket aircraft, helicopters, hovercraft and even cars and motorbikes.

Alliot died in 1958 aged 80. He is buried in the churchyard of the parish church of St Andrew, in Hamble. His family is still very much in touch with developments at Vulcan to the Sky Trust and has seen XH558 display recently.

Major Players
in the design of Avro 698

The company of Avro and their ultimate success in gaining contract to begin production of the Avro 698 was really the result of two key people who joined Alliot in his endeavours, just on the outbreak of World War 1. With their help, in only ten short years, Avro would become one of Britain's largest engineering concerns, at the forefront of the new sector that was to become known as aeronautical design.

Firstly, there was their highly talented forward thinking designer, Roy Chadwick. Then, a man of immense business acumen in the form of Roy Dobson, who became Avro's General Manager and sat as Managing Director during the majority of the Vulcan programme. Between them, they moulded the company in the inter-war years, making it one of the leading aircraft companies in the world and a driving force behind Britain's excellence and internationally renowned reputation as a leading aeronautical power.

We profile here a brief background of all the main players involved in the design and building of Avro Vulcan aircraft, from the early development 707s through the prototypes, to the final Mk.2 production aircraft.

The Avro 698 prototype. *BAE*

Roy Chadwick CBE, FRAeS - Chief Designer to Technical Director

Roy Chadwick was born in 1893 in Widnes in Cheshire, the son of a mechanical engineer. At just 18 years of age in 1911, he began working at Avro as an assistant to A.V. Roe and became quickly involved in working closely on Avro's latest designs in the drawing office.

His talent and vision were quickly recognised by Alliot and he encouraged him to take up specific projects of his own, resulting in several models named simply in alphabetical order of Avro D, E and F. The first two were really just adaptations of earlier machines, taking a bi-plane to a seaplane, but it was with the Avro F, the world's first monoplane with an enclosed cabin, by which he cemented his reputation as a true innovator.

By the end of World War II, Roy had designed perhaps the most famous of all Avro aircraft - the Avro Lancaster. Just over five years from its first flight in 1941, he would sketch out the radical Delta concept for a new Air Ministry specification that pushed the boundaries of weight, altitude and range to unheard of levels, way beyond the capabilities of any known aircraft at that time.

After initial planning and evaluation, it was Chadwick that would confirm the decision to go ahead with tender documents on the basis of the pure Delta, and he would hand over the project to Stuart Davies, to concentrate on a civil version of the Lancaster - the Avro Tudor. Sadly, it was when the early Mark II prototype Tudor crashed at Woodford in 1947 due to incorrectly connected control wires, that Chadwick and three others lost their lives. He was never to see his brainchild of a Delta aircraft take flight.

Verne Morse

Roy Hardy Dobson - Trainee Draftsman to Managing Director

Born in 1891 in Horsworth, near Leeds, Roy joined the company as a draftsman in 1914 and worked in the drawing offices through until 1919, by which time he had not only grasped a solid aeronautical engineering base, but had become adept with excellent communication skills and a thorough understanding of the importance of cost analysis as the company grew and needed to deal with the ever increasing number of suppliers.

His rise through the ranks to boardroom level was swift and mirrored the fast pace of development in aircraft design by his contemporaries. It was experience that would give him excellent negotiation skills, significant in the tendering process and presentations favoured by successive governments as the number of available aircraft manufacturers increased and competed against one-another for the many and varied contracts of the era.

He was also responsible for establishing the Avro division in Canada during 1945, with the plan to build aircraft under licence, or to service existing aircraft coming back from the war effort. It was only a matter of years, with the transfer of pooled talent and key local appointments that the division would set up its own design offices and manufacturing base, leading to quite a diverse range of aircraft to that of its parent.

Eventually becoming Chairman of the enlarged Hawker Siddeley Group, Roy was knighted for his services to industry, only retiring in 1967 at the age of 76. He died a little over a year later.

Stuart Duncan Davies CBE, FEng, FRAeS - Assistant, then Chief Designer

Born in 1906 in North London, Stuart started work at the age of 16 with Vauxhall Motors, where he stayed for two years before moving on to work in the fascinating new world of aircraft design by joining Vickers as a technical assistant. Studying Engineering, he gained a BSc and worked at Brooklands in their wind tunnel on early aircraft designs. By 1931, he had moved to Hawker Aircraft where he worked on Hart and Fury biplanes, which were the RAF's main fighter aircraft of the period. The last aircraft would soon become a monoplane and in 1933, he started work on what would become better known as the Hawker Hurricane. With the merger of Hawker, his talents became known to others in the group, particularly over at A V Roe, who enticed him over with the position of assistant to the Chief Designer (the renowned Roy Chadwick) which proved to be all the incentive he needed. By late 1939, he had established his reputation and was promoted to be the company's experimental manager being assigned responsibility under Roy to convert the Manchester aircraft into the soon to be named Avro Lancaster.

Avro Heritage

Impressed with his work and the resultant aircraft, Roy promoted him to Chief Designer, moving his own position up to that of Technical Director, leaving the way forward for him to concentrate on the civilian conversion of the Lancaster and initial design work of a new radical delta shape. With the tragic loss of Roy in 1947, Stuart suddenly found himself thrust to new challenges and even more responsibility.

He left Avro in 1955, when he was succeeded by Roy Ewans, although he returned to Hawker Siddeley Aviation in the early sixties, before finally retiring. A few years later, in 1968 he was awarded the CBE for his services to industry. He died in January 1995 aged 88.

Roy Ewans - Aerodynamicist to Chief Designer

Born in 1917 in Torquay, Roy won a scholarship to St Paul's School. He graduated from Imperial College, London with a First in Mechanical Engineering, before taking a postgraduate diploma in Aeronautical Engineering. In 1939, Ewans joined the Royal Aircraft Establishment at Farnborough and worked on various research projects. After the war, he joined the Blackburn Aircraft Company before moving to Avro in 1949, working on the latter stages of the 707 proof of concept aircraft and the prototype 698 design.

Even as the first B1 Vulcans rolled off the production line, it became clear that advances in Soviet fighter design would mean they could soon reach the same planned cruise altitudes of 50,000ft plus. Roy's knowledge led to the development of a redesigned wing shape and an increased wingspan that would increase lift and manoeuvrability at higher altitudes. With this was born the B2.

By 1961, his work on Vulcans complete, Ewans had left Avro to move to the newly-formed British Aircraft Corporation. In 1967 he joined Fairchild in the USA where he worked as project engineer on the development of a small passenger jet. He was also involved in advanced helicopter rotor research before becoming chief engineer on the S340 passenger aircraft in collaboration with SAAB.

Ewans retired in 1982 and lived for a while at St Mawes in Cornwall, where he pursued his interest in sailing. Later, he later moved to Poole and then to Virginia Water. He was elected a Fellow of the Royal Aeronautical Society in 1957. Sadly, Roy died in January of 2012 at the age of 94.

Roland 'Roly' John Falk OBE, AFC

Born in London in 1915 and educated at Stowe School and the de Havilland Technical School, Roland Falk flew in both the Abyssinian War and the Spanish Civil War for the press, and flew a newspaper service from London to Paris before joining the Air Registration Board as a test pilot. In 1939, at the start of World War II, he joined the Royal Air Force and by 1943 was chief test pilot at the Royal Aircraft Establishment Farnborough, flying and testing captured German aircraft and carrying out operational flights with night fighter squadrons.

In 1946 he joined Vickers Armstrong but was severely injured in an accident in a Wellington. Once recovered he went to Avro, initially to test fly the Avro Athena, before taking on one of the most important jobs of his career, test pilot of the experimental delta-winged Avro 707. Falk then piloted the Avro 698 prototype on its first flight on 30 August 1952, subsequently demonstrating the Vulcan on several occasions. Notoriously, during the 1955 Farnborough Airshow he barrel-rolled a Vulcan which, although safe, was a spectacular manoeuvre in an aircraft of such size, and one the authorities requested he did not repeat!

Falk was appointed an Officer of the Order of the British Empire in 1952, and retired from Avro in 1958. He was a sales representative for Hawker Siddeley for a while until he set up his own aircraft business in Jersey, where he died on 23 February 1985 aged 69.

Samuel Eric 'Red' Esler DFC

Born in Belfast in 1918, Eric Esler was educated at Skegoniel School and Belfast College of Technology. He was commissioned in May 1942 and flew Liberators in No. 120 Squadron, Coastal Command, being awarded the DFC in December 1942.

Esler joined A.V. Roe in June 1948, and as deputy chief test pilot was made responsible for flying the Type 707, due to the absence in Canada of Avro's chief test pilot, J.H. Orrell. The 707 began taxiing trials at Boscombe Down on September 3rd 1949, and during one of these tests made a short hop a few feet above the ground. The first flight took place the following evening, when Esler flew the aircraft for twenty minutes. Two days later, on 6 September, the 707 arrived at Farnborough for static exhibition at the SBAC Display. On 30 September, VX784 was on a flight from the Royal Aircraft Establishment when Esler lost control at low speed near Blackbushe and was killed. The aircraft was almost totally destroyed by fire, the probable cause of the crash being a sudden control circuit failure causing the air brakes to be locked open, thus provoking a stall.

James 'Jimmy' Gordon Harrison OBE, AFC

James Gordon Harrison was born on December 22 1918 at Portsmouth. A graduate of the Empire Test Pilots' School and night fighter pilot for the RAF, Harrison was appointed to the prestigious Aeroflight at Farnborough, where he flew many of the experimental aircraft being developed at the time, and was awarded the Air Force Cross for his work. His exceptional skills drew the attention of Avro's chief test pilot, Roly Falk, and he joined the company in 1953, eventually succeeding Falk as Chief Test Pilot in 1958. His arrival coincided with a difficult phase of the development of the Vulcan, and he spent much of 1954 testing one of the Avro 707As.

Harrison had his share of emergencies in what was then an inherently risky profession (10 of the 28 pilots on his test pilot course were to lose their lives). On July 24 1959 he took off in a Vulcan with a crew of five at Woodford. The aircraft suffered a complete electrical failure and with every attempt to save the aircraft having failed Harrison climbed to gain enough height for the three rear crew members to successfully bale out. He then headed for the Humber estuary before he and his co-pilot ejected.

Harrison flew almost 8,000 hours on 93 different aircraft types during his career, including no fewer than 13 different prototypes. He retired from flying in 1969, his final job at Avro being product support manager, a post he held for 14 years. In 1968 he was appointed OBE for his key role in developing the Vulcan, and also received two Queen's Commendations for Valuable Services in the Air. He died on April 16 2007.

James 'Jimmy' C. Nelson AFC

Jimmy Nelson was born in Colorado, USA in 1919 and learned to fly while at university. He came to England in July 1941 and served in the RAF's No. 133 Squadron, one of three 'Eagle' squadrons comprised of United States nationals who wished to fight before their country had entered hostilities.

In 1942, rather than transfer to the USAAF, Nelson stayed in the RAF where he commanded special high-altitude Spitfire Mk VI aircraft. He then went to RAE Farnborough as a test pilot in 1943. In March 1944 he had a bad crash in a Mosquito when an engine failed at only 200ft. He broke 30 bones and later lost a leg as a result of his injuries, but returned to the RAE on the Jet Development Flight. He joined Avro in 1948 after three years as a test pilot for Miles Aircraft. Besides the Avro 707 he flew the Ashton, Shackleton and Athena but then returned to the USA in 1953. He died in 1989.

Jack Bertram Wales OBE, DFC, TD

Jack Wales was born in January, 1917. He joined the Army in 1936 and was seconded to the Royal Air Force in 1940, serving as a fighter pilot in India and the Far East. Before the war, he had worked in A.V. Roe's experimental department and he rejoined the firm as a production pilot two years after the war. He performed the arduous research flying in the Avro 707 aircraft, making the maiden flight of Avro 707C WZ744 on 1st July 1953. Squadron Leader Wales was killed on the 7th December 1956 when the prototype Avro Shackleton Mk3 (WR970) crashed whilst on a test flight from Woodford, killing all on board.

Tony Blackman OBE

Tony Blackman was educated at Oundle School and Trinity College Cambridge, where he obtained an honours degree in Physics. He learnt to fly in the RAF, and flew Vampire and Venom jet fighters in Germany. He trained as a test pilot at the Empire Test Pilots School, and from there tested V-Bombers at Boscombe Down. As a result he was recruited by Roly Falk in 1956. Tony spent 22 years at Avro, becoming Chief Test Pilot from 1970 to 1978, and flying 105 of the 136 Vulcans built, as well as a 707A when developing the auto throttle for the Vulcan. Besides developing the Vulcan and the Nimrod, he spent many years testing, developing and demonstrating the Avro 748 all round the World. He received the Queens Commendation for Valuable Services in the Air and later was awarded an OBE.

As an expert in aviation electronics he was invited by Smiths Industries to join their Aerospace Board, initially as technical operations director, helping develop the new large electronic displays and flight management systems. On leaving Smiths he joined the board of the UK Civil Aviation Authority. He now lives in Hamble with his wife Margaret and has written several books, including 'Vulcan Test Pilot'.

The Avro Vulcan strategic bomber was born of the atomic age and the Cold War. The detonation of nuclear weapons over the Japanese cities of Hiroshima and Nagasaki demonstrated that all previous defence planning was futile. Only the power to destroy an enemy city under a mushroom cloud would be sufficient to protect Britain, and from the first atomic weapons policy onwards the nuclear strategy focussed on deterrence.

In November 1945 a government committee concluded that securing an international agreement banning the production of nuclear weapons would be impossible - the genie was out of the bottle. The decision was taken that Britain had to have the bomb, despite reservations from some ministers that the cash-strapped country could not afford it. Foreign Secretary Ernest Bevin put it bluntly: "We've got to have this thing over here, whatever it costs. We've got to have the bloody Union Jack on top of it." The formal decision to become a nuclear power was taken in January 1947 by a top secret Cabinet Committee, chaired by the Prime Minister Clement Attlee.

It was obvious to military strategists that any future bomber to deliver a nuclear weapon would have to be jet powered and of advanced aerodynamic design. The RAF was aware that its front-line bombers, the Lancaster, Lincoln and Washington (American B-29s) were effectively obsolete, and on New Year's Day 1947 specification B.35/46 (based on the Air Staff's Operational Requirement 229) was issued to the aircraft industry by the Ministry of Supply (MoS). This called for a high-altitude, high-speed, strategic bomber capable of delivering a single 10,000 lb (4,536 kg) nuclear weapon to a target 1,725 miles (2,780 km) distant. Six companies, Vickers, Handley Page, Armstrong Whitworth, English Electric, Short Brothers and Avro, submitted tenders in May 1947.

A six man Avro design team led by Chief Designer Stuart Davies and overseen by Technical Director Roy Chadwick started initially with a conventional layout with swept wings, but by progressively shortening the fuselage and then removing the tailplane, a delta-wing planform emerged.

Above: The Hiroshima bomb. Below: The prototype Messerschmitt 163, that showed a tailless design was feasible. Below right: Early concept sketches for the Avro 698 planform.

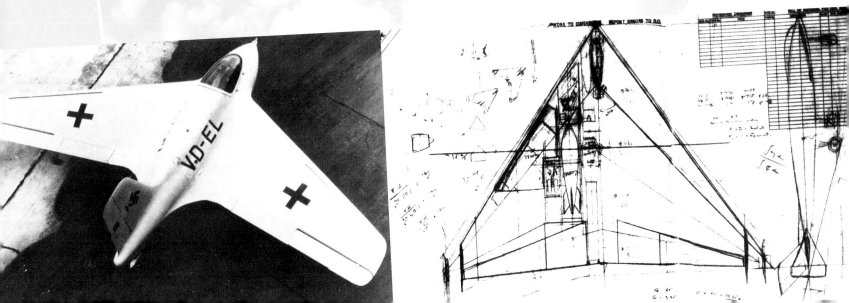

This was a bold step by the designers because little was known about delta aerodynamics at the time, and the concept of the 'flying triangle' of these proportions was a daunting prospect. Designers in Britain, the USA and France had made some studies of a delta configuration, but the outbreak of World War II had largely put such research on hold. Germany, under designers like Dr Alexander Lippisch and the Horten brothers was more advanced, and post-war America was able to take advantage of captured scientists including Lippisch to further their own projects. British manufacturers, on the other hand, only had the data from RAE evaluations of captured Messerschmitt 262 and 163 aircraft. However, by March 1947 Chadwick had made a firm decision to go ahead with the delta configuration, with the tender documents being confirmed in a meeting with the MoS on 28 July.

All the designs were passed to the Royal Aircraft Establishment at Farnborough for evaluation, and the Advanced Bomber Project Group was set up for this purpose, under the RAE's Head of Aerodynamic Flight Section, Morien Morgan (later to find fame on the Concorde project). The six were whittled down to two, the Avro 698 and Handley Page HP80, though as both were at the cutting edge of aircraft design the ABPG recommended that a less advanced alternative should also be commissioned. This would allow the introduction of a jet bomber into RAF service sooner than would be possible with the other two. As a result, Vickers tendered designs for the Valiant, a development of their original 35/46 tender, and the first prototype, WB210, flew on 18 May 1951.

The Avro team suffered a grievous loss with the death of Roy Chadwick, who was killed in the crash of the Tudor 2 prototype at Woodford on 23 August 1947. Assistant Chief Designer S.D. Davies, who had survived the accident, now took over design leadership of the delta programme, and Chadwick's post as Technical Director was taken by William S. Farren, a former director of RAE Farnborough and a man of the highest reputation in aeronautics.

The tender for the Avro 698 was accepted by the MoS on 27 November 1947, and the Instruction to Proceed for the production of two prototypes came on 1 January 1948. In the weeks before, extensive wind tunnel testing at RAE Farnborough had led to considerable evolution of the design; initially the payload was to be carried in the wings, with the engines in superimposed pairs, but the testing highlighted the need for a thinner wing resulting in a central bomb-bay and engines repositioned in side-by-side pairs. A forward fuselage was added, as was a conventional rear tailfin and rudder to replace the originally proposed movable wingtips. The Vulcan as we know it was emerging.

Left: The first of the one-third scale Type 707s, VX784, built to research the delta planform.

Below: An early model of the Type 698. *BAE Woodford*

The ABPG had recommended that further research be conducted into the delta planform, research that would require the construction of aircraft to test the wing at high and low airspeeds and various altitudes up to the specified ceiling of 50,000ft. Avro therefore began construction of the one-third scale Type 707s, the first of which was designed for low speed trials (see page 84 for more details on the type). Work on VX784 commenced in mid 1948 and was completed in August 1949 at Woodford. After ground running and taxiing trials the aircraft was dismantled and shipped to the Aeroplane and Armament Experimental Establishment

Above: Avro Type 698 takes off on its maiden flight from Woodford. *Cyril Peckham*

Below: A tight fit; the centre section of a Vulcan makes its way to Woodford from Chadderton for assembly. *BAE Woodford*

(A&AEE) at Boscombe Down, then being reassembled in readiness for flight. First flight took place on 4 September in the hands of Flight Lieutenant Eric S. Esler, with two more flights made before the aircraft was flown to Farnborough for static display at the Society of British Aerospace Companies (SBAC) show.

Thus far, the flight characteristics of the 707 had been unremarkable, so on 30 September it came as a considerable shock to Avro when the aircraft crashed, killing Esler. Nonetheless, construction of the second 707, VX790, proceeded as planned, and in August 1950 it was taken by road to Boscombe Down, where on 6 September it made its maiden flight piloted by Wing Commander Roly Falk, who had recently joined Avro as chief test pilot. The speed trials that followed revealed that the unusual dorsal air intake suffered from air starvation at high speed, and the following 707s were all constructed with wing root intakes. One of these, designated Type 707A, was to be the high-speed aircraft to provide data on the upper reaches of the delta flight envelope, but by now work on the 698 was overtaking the 707 programme, in part due to the Avro design office being stretched by work on the Shackleton that Coastal Command was desperate for. This would have a significant impact on the Vulcan planform further down the line.

The 707 had vindicated the delta design concept, and in the meantime the Type 698 was taking shape, the mighty wing being built at Woodford with the rest of the airframe constructed at Chadderton. Its intended engines, the Bristol BE 10 (Olympus) had run for the first time at Patchway

on 6 May 1950, producing 11,000lb of thrust, but with ground runs still ongoing in 1952 Avro chose Rolls-Royce Avons to power the prototype. The sections built at Chadderton were transported by road (not without some difficulty) to Woodford for final assembly, with Avro keen to have the aircraft ready for the 1952 SBAC show, not least to beat their rivals Handley Page. In the last week of August VX770 emerged from the Woodford assembly hangar, having taken just 28 months to build, and ground running trials proceeded apace.

On 30 August 1952 VX770 was ready for its first flight, in the very capable hands of Avro's chief test pilot. Roly Falk described the occasion: "It was a large aircraft and was, of course, unlike anything of its size which had flown before. My experience on the 707s had, however, given me the greatest confidence. One fast taxi run was sufficient to satisfy me with regard to ground handling, wheel shimmy and nosewheel lifting speed. A short run and the aircraft lifted smoothly into the air, the undercarriage up when well clear of the ground in case of any unexpected change in trim and a climb to about 10,000ft, some preliminary manoeuvres in order to get the feel of the controls and that was sufficient for the first flight."

The only snag on the flight was that both fairing panels behind the main undercarriage fell away when the wheels were lowered for landing, and the prototype subsequently flew without these for several weeks until a series of modifications were carried out. The required flying hours were completed just in time to allow an appearance in the air at the SBAC show, with the Type 698 making five flights over the week. Accompanied by two 707s, VX790 in blue and WD280 in red, the all-white 698 was a dramatic sight and unsurprisingly received enthusiastic headlines in the press. Shortly after, it received its name - Chief of Air Staff Sir John Slessor decided that both the Handley Page and Avro bombers were to begin with 'V' - the Vulcan was born.

Above: The immaculate Roly Falk stands in front of the second Avro 698 prototype, impatient to get started! *Cyril Peckham*

Below: The two 698 prototypes, together at Farnborough in 1953, VX777 leading. *Barry Jones*

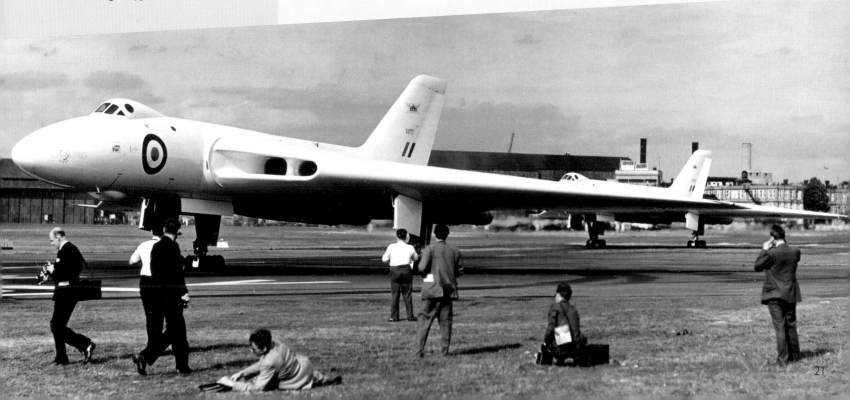

In May 1953 VX770 was fitted with 7,500lb thrust Armstrong Siddeley Sapphire turbojets for high-speed high-altitude trials, as the Olympus powerplants were not yet operational. The second prototype, VX777, was nearing completion, and featured a longer nose and bomb-aimers blister, and would finally receive the 9,750lb thrust Bristol Olympus Mk 100. Falk had considerable input on the cockpit instrument layout, and at his suggestion the conventional control wheel that had been used on VX770 was replaced with a fighter-style control stick. The maiden flight took place on 3 September 1953, and the aircraft appeared a few days later at Farnborough accompanied by sister aircraft VX770 and all four Avro 707s.

A comprehensive programme of system trials was underway by the spring of 1954, but Vulcan trials then suffered a severe blow when VX777 was badly damaged in a heavy landing at Farnborough. Avro continued the programme as best it could with VX770, finally commencing high-speed, high-altitude trials, and now the delays that had seen the Type 698 overtake the 707 programme bit hard. Trials with the 707A had recently revealed the airframe vibrated badly at high speed and altitude, and this data was confirmed by VX770. Airflow was separating from the outer wing upper surfaces, causing a compressibility stall between 0.8 and 0.85M, well below the speed that could be achieved by Olympus-powered Vulcans. Avro experimented with vortex generators and wing fences, but the only solution would be to redesign the leading edge of the wing.

The straight edged wing was swept at a constant 52 degree angle; this was decreased by 10 degrees at mid span, then brought back to 52 degrees further outboard, adding a slight droop at the same time. The design was tested on the Type 707 WD280 in 1954 and succeeded in pushing back the compressibility buffet beyond the speeds and altitudes that would be encountered by the Vulcan. The solution came at a price though. All leading edges already on the production jigs had to be scrapped, and the jigs themselves rebuilt. Additionally, the solution came too late to be incorporated into the first production Vulcan B1, XA889, completed in January 1955. Shortly after, a repaired VX777 rejoined the test programme, and after being given the new leading edge in July it became the first to begin flight trials with what was now known as the Phase 2 wing. By now two production Vulcans were flying, XA889 being joined by XA890, the latter gaining notoriety for performing an upward barrel roll in the hands of Roly Falk at the 1955 SBAC show.

VX770 and XA889 underwent acceptance trials at A&AEE, and the Vulcan was cleared for entry into RAF service on 29 May 1956, with the first B1 (XA897) delivered to 230 Operational Conversion Unit at RAF Waddington on 20 July. Several of the initial production batch had been allocated to development and testing programmes and in fact 230 OCU only had their hands on XA897 briefly before it was returned to Woodford for modifications and replaced by XA895.

The reason for XA897s withdrawal soon became clear. The modifications included the installation of bomb-bay fuel tanks, increasing the aircraft's range by 700 miles. On 9 September 1956 it took off from Boscombe Down for the long flight to New Zealand and Australia to take part in a display for Air Force Commemoration Week. The trip was viewed as a valuable opportunity to promote and prove the aircraft, being the first long-range flight the Vulcan had undertaken. A crew hand-picked for their experience and skill had been assembled, captained by Squadron Leader Donald Howard, with the Commander in Chief of Bomber Command, Air Marshal Sir Harry Broadhurst as co-pilot. All the remaining three RAF crew were Squadron Leaders, with one civilian aboard, Avro technical service representative Frederick Bassett. The outbound flight went smoothly, with the 11,475 mile distance to Melbourne covered in 47 hours 26 minutes including stopovers at Aden and Singapore, a total flight time of just 23 hours 9 minutes. Broadhurst took the opportunity to point out to Australian ministers that neither their front-line fighter, the American Sabre, nor any similar type would be able to catch the Vulcan!

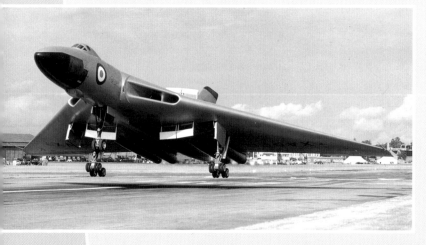

Below: Second production Vulcan XA890 in silver finish at Farnborough in 1955, note the early twin under-wing airbrakes. *Barry Jones*

After visits to Sydney, Adelaide and Christchurch New Zealand the long return flight began. In the early morning of 1 October the Vulcan departed from Aden on the last leg, Broadhurst in the co-pilot seat and alternating with Howard at the controls. A VIP reception at London Heathrow Airport eagerly awaited the arrival, though poor weather surrounded the area with rain and mist. The first thing the waiting crowds were aware of was the sound of a burst of full power, followed by the Vulcan climbing steeply to about 800ft, where the cockpit canopy released and the two forward crew ejector seats fired. The aircraft then dived to starboard, crashing on the edge of Runway Four where it exploded on impact, killing the four rear crew members.

What had started out as a demonstration of the new aircraft's capabilities turned into a publicity nightmare, making headlines around the world for all the wrong reasons. The Daily Mirror's report on 2 October described the incident: "A mist-shrouded cabbage field sealed the fate of the £1,000,000 four-jet Avro Vulcan which crashed and burned out yesterday. The giant bomber, being 'talked down' to London Airport by radar through torrential rain and mist, undershot the runway by 600 yards and its landing wheels hit the cabbage field. They were ripped off. Immediately, the pilot put 'full power' on the four jet engines and the aircraft roared into a steep climb. But as it went into the low cloud, the pilot realised it was out of control..." Subsequent investigation absolved the aircraft and blamed a culmination of errors, including RAE evidence that suggested altimeter friction and extra pressure error could make the instrument read incorrectly by as much as 200ft.

The loss of XA897 left 230 OCU with just one aircraft, until the arrival of XA898 in January 1957. Three more aircraft were on strength soon after, allowing the first OCU course to graduate on 20 May. Pilots and co-pilots came from a tour on Canberras, experienced in flying jets at high speeds and altitudes, and once used to the Vulcan's size had little difficulty adapting to the big delta. OCU training started with four weeks of ground school, and towards the end of this pilots would spend 16 hours on the flight simulator, before moving to mixed ground school and flying for two weeks. The final phase was an intense six weeks of flying, by the end of which pilots would have around 50 hours on type, half of it at night.

Navigator Plotters and Navigators Radar also often came from Canberras, though some had experience on Lincolns or Washingtons. The new systems on the Vulcan meant their workload was high, with the 'Green Satin' radar aid and new bombing systems with H2S radar to master. The third crew member, the Air Electronics Officer, was a new category, and the course was possibly the most intensive of all with a great deal of electronic theory to absorb. This would stand them in good stead as electronic countermeasures began to emerge, systems that would double an AEO's workload in operational conditions!

Below: The RAF were proud of their new acquisition, as can be seen from these adverts.

Opposite page: Two Vulcans near the Hoover Dam, 1959. *Ralph Crane/Time & Life Pictures/Getty Images*

Duck and cover! Vulcans demonstrate a bomb run in Nevada, 1959, led by XH502 of 617 Squadron.
Ralph Crane/Time & Life Pictures/Getty Images

From the time of their arrival into service at the OCU, all the Vulcans were painted silver, but in April 1957 the first wearing the all-new white colour scheme arrived, and the earlier aircraft were gradually repainted. The first operational Vulcan unit was 'A' Flight of 83 Squadron at RAF Waddington, formed by the first OCU graduates. Their first Vulcan, XA905, was delivered on 11 July 1957, and by the end of the year they had received five more. The aircraft, in anti-flash white and bearing the City of Lincoln shield on their fins were worked hard, their crews carrying out an intensive training programme that included long-range overseas flights. This included the Vulcan's first participation in what was to be an annual event for the V-Force, the Strategic Air Command's Bombing, Navigation and Reconnaissance Competition.

In early 1958 the Squadron was chosen to carry out a series of overseas goodwill tours, some as 'Lone Rangers' where the crew would have to carry out minor servicing and tail parachute repacking themselves. Travelling to, and displaying at a variety of locations in Africa and South America the trips were a resounding success, typical of prestige flights Vulcans would undertake in the years to come, enhancing the aircraft's reputation as a global bomber. Tragedy struck again though, with the loss of two aircraft in the space of a month, the first being the prototype VX770 which crashed at a Battle of Britain display at Syerston on 20 September, killing all four crew and three airmen on the ground. Then on 24 October XA908 suffered total electrical failure on a 'Lone Ranger' from Goose bay to Lincoln, Nebraska, crashing in a suburb of Detroit. All six crew were lost, but miraculously only one person on the ground was seriously hurt.

By now several more Vulcan squadrons had entered service; 101 Squadron re-formed at Finningley on 15 October 1957, and had been joined by the famous 'Dam Busters', 617 Squadron at Scampton on 1 May 1958. 617's first Vulcan, XH482 was delivered from Woodford by Air Commodore J.N.H. 'Charles' Whitworth, the Scampton Station Commander at the time of the 1943 dams raid.

Apart from overseas tours there were, of course, exercises to simulate the 'real thing'. The V-Force relied on the tactic of dispersing to airfields around the country to escape enemy attacks directed at its main bases, and alert exercises could happen at any time, sometimes with prior notice, sometimes not (the latter known by the codename 'Mickey Finn'). In an exercise the degree of alert would progressively increase, and at Readiness Zero Two engines were started, and aircraft in groups of four would scramble to their dispersal fields, or sometimes go straight into a training profile. Once at dispersal the Vulcans could be scrambled at a moment's notice. Air and ground crews might have to spend days living in caravans close to their aircraft waiting for the call, the ground crews having to carry out full pre-take-off checks every 24 hours.

Test beds and drawing board

Aside from regular duties, several Vulcan airframes were put to use in test and development roles. XA894 spent all its life as a test aircraft, and was delivered to Filton in 1960, where the Olympus 22R (intended to power the TSR2) was fitted into the bomb-bay. An engine explosion during ground running in December 1962 unfortunately destroyed the aircraft.

Probably one of the most famous Vulcans after XH558 was the B1, XA903. This aircraft never entered operational service, but played a significant role in aeronautic development from the 1950s through to the '70s. Completed in 1957, the 15th airframe built by Avro at Woodford, it was initially used for trials of the Blue Steel missile (and was the only B1 ever to carry it).

Above: XA894 with underslung Olympus 22 engine, as part of the test programme for the TSR2.
Rolls-Royce

It then became an engine test-bed at Filton for the Rolls-Royce/Snecma Olympus 593 engine that was to power Concorde. The engine was installed as one half of a Concorde nacelle, attached underneath the bomb-bay space. The bomb bay space was used for additional fuel tanks that were used to supply the 593 engine, and for a water tank that was used as part of the engine tests. A water spray grid was fitted in front of the nacelle for de-icing trials. This contained over a hundred nozzles spraying water into the engine at varying flow rates to test the operation of intake de-icing system.

XA903 with Olympus 593. The spray rig can be clearly seen in front of the nacelle, as can the protective shielding around the Vulcan's tail.
Rolls-Royce

The vast array of sensors fitted to the 593 required an external wiring loom to be fitted down the port side of the aircraft, and the rear cabin was unique to XA903 - a large instrument panel that contained over 100 instruments and indicators was installed on the starboard side of the rear desk. The final 593 flight test took place in July 1971 and in August aircraft went to Marshall's of Cambridge for conversion to carry the RB199 destined for the Panavia Tornado. The forebody of the engine nacelle had been designed to provide two 27mm Mauser cannon positions together with ammunition stowage for 150 shells. XA903 thus became the only cannon-armed Vulcan with several gun firing trials carried out on the butts at Boscombe Down, and over the Irish Sea.

During these trials XA903 began to show her age. The last RAF B1 had been withdrawn in 1968 and spares were in short supply, sometimes resulting in gate guardians being 'robbed' for parts. In 1977 the aircraft became the only in-service Vulcan to be totally re-wired, an impressive feat as the wiring was 'built-in' and not designed to be replaced. In August 1978, the RB199 trials were completed and XA903 was allocated to Farnborough for ground training. The aircraft was scrapped in 1984, with the nose section preserved in private ownership.

Two concepts that never left the drawing board were the Avro Atlantic passenger jet and the Vulcan Phase 6. Roy Chadwick had doodled a delta winged transport aircraft as early as 1947, and in 1952 while the 698 was being developed design investigation on the Atlantic, designated the Type 722, began. It was described in Popular Mechanics, October 1953 as: "A development of the Avro Vulcan... Its delta-wing design will put the

Below left: The RB199 engine nacelle fitted to XA903. *Avro* Below right: The Avro Atlantic airliner. *Popular Mechanics*

exhaust ends of the four turbojet engines, where the noise is highest, well behind the rear passenger seats. All passenger seats will face the rear, an arrangement recommended by many safety experts". The design progressed no further than drawings and a few models.

The Phase 6, or B3, was to be a larger, more powerful version of the Vulcan, powered by Olympus 23s and capable of carrying six Skybolt missiles, but concept work was abandoned soon after the Skybolt programme was cancelled at the end of 1962. Some consideration was even given to a vertical take-off Vulcan, with ten B 59 lift engines fitted in the bomb-bay, but the idea was dropped as the weight penalty would have been enormous.

Enter the B2

In 1955 Avro's new Chief Designer, Roy Ewans and his team had been working on redesigning the Mk.1 airframe to increase the lift and manoeuvrability at the heights the Vulcan would be capable of with the increasingly powerful variants of the Olympus engine. The Phase 2 wing was increased in span from 99ft to 111ft, and wing area from 3,446sq ft to 3,965sq ft, which in conjunction with the new Olympus 200 would not only boost performance at altitude, but also increase range and operational ceiling. The MoS approved the Phase 2C design and in March 1956 issued the contract to convert VX777 into the prototype B2, placing a production order for the B2 in June. Production of the B1 was halted with XH532, and the remaining 25 B1s on contract would be completed to B2 standard.

VX777 was fitted with Olympus 102 engines of 12,000lb thrust and the Phase 2C wing, which replaced the elevators and ailerons of the Mk.1 with full-span elevons, and first flew in the new configuration on 31 August 1957 as it entered aerodynamic trials. The B2 design featured other significant modifications, including a less bulky 200-volt AC electrical system, Lucas Auxiliary Airborne Power Plant (AAPP), enlarged air intakes and strengthened undercarriage with a shorter nose leg. The first aircraft to fly with these refinements was the pre-production XH533 on 19 August 1958, and it later demonstrated the effectiveness of the new wing by climbing to 61,500ft.

A practice scramble at RAF Scampton in 1960. Popperfoto/Getty Images

With the development programme well underway Avro received an instruction to fit new ECM equipment, including the Red Steer tail warning radar, involving a redesign of the entire rear fuselage below the fin to accommodate it. The B2's new tailcone increased the overall length by nearly 3 feet, and a flat aerial plate was installed between the starboard jet pipes.

XH534 underwent Controller Aircraft clearance trials at Boscombe Down, and the B2 received clearance in May 1960, the first into service being XH558, which was delivered to 230 OCU on 1 July. There were still 34 B1s in RAF service and it had been decided to fit the best of these with the ECM kit used in the B2 - no simple task as the DC electrics on the B1 couldn't be completely modified to AC and an engine-driven alternator had to be installed. Work was mainly carried out by Armstrong Whitworth, who completed the conversion of 29 aircraft, now designated B1A, in 32 months. At around this time, a further modification was introduced to the fleet in the form of in-flight refuelling capability, increasing mission range and flight time. Several Valiant bombers were converted to the tanker role.

All the B1 and 1As were now concentrated in three squadrons at Waddington; No 44 (Rhodesia) Squadron re-formed in August 1960, taking over 83 Squadron's eight B1s, and was joined by 101 Squadron which brought its five B1s and two B1As down from Finningley, swapping places with 230 OCU. The third squadron was No 50 which re-formed in August 1961, taking B1s from 617.

Scampton was reorganised to accommodate three B2 squadrons; No 83 arrived in the Autumn of 1960 and took delivery of their first B2 in December. In April 1961 they were joined by a re-formed 27 Squadron, and finally 617 received their first B2 in September to replace the B1s given to 50 Squadron. In 1962 a second B2 wing was established at RAF Coningsby, with three disbanded Canberra squadrons re-formed, No IX, No 12 and No 35. The latter received B2s from the Scampton squadrons which were receiving new aircraft modified to carry Blue Steel.

Blue Steel was a rocket-propelled nuclear standoff missile, carried partly recessed into the bomb-bay of Vulcan and Victor aircraft and was capable of supersonic cruise speeds. Work on the weapon had begun in 1956 when Avro received a development contract from the MoS. The first test firing took place at the Woomera rocket range in Australia early in 1961 and, by early 1963, 617 Squadron became the first fully operational unit to be equipped, followed by 27 and 83 Squadrons later that year. Together with 100 and 139 Squadron Victors they

Top: RAF Finningley on 28th July 1965. Left to right, XH558, XH556, XA900, XA901, XH563 and XH537, B1 aircraft in white and B2s in camouflage.
F.W. Elliot

Above: A Blue Steel missile being lowered into its 'dolly' from a transportation vehicle.
Crown Copyright/IWM

formed the spearhead of the nuclear deterrent, with aircraft on Quick Reaction Alert (QRA) aiming to be airborne within 90 seconds of starting to roll.

Even while Blue Steel was undergoing tests, its intended replacement was well advanced, the RAF having shown an interest in the American Skybolt missile back in 1959. This was designed to have a range of over 1,000 miles as against Blue Steel's 100, and a Vulcan would be capable of carrying two, one under each wing. In March 1960 agreement was reached with the Americans to supply the RAF, with a target in service date of the end of 1963. Accordingly, 40 Vulcan B2s were modified with strengthened wings and Skybolt attachment points (which were later to prove useful in the Falklands conflict for carrying Shrike missiles and the Westinghouse ECM pod), and XH537 flew with a pair of dummy missiles on wing pylons in November 1961.

Tests of the missile were problematic, and this, together with escalating costs and the arrival of the United States Navy's Polaris missile, led to the US cancelling Skybolt at the end of 1962. With the British government's planned basis for its entire nuclear deterrent removed at a stroke, Prime Minister Harold Macmillan opted for the submarine-launched Polaris. This would enter service at the end of the decade, the V-Force shouldering the nuclear deterrent role until then.

Scampton squadrons had taken part in a number of exercises simulating war conditions, one of the most remarkable being Exercise Skyshield II in October 1961. Skyshield was designed to test the North American Air Defense Command and its chains of early warning radar, interceptors and ground-to-air missiles by launching a series of 'saturation' attacks by USAF bombers acting as hostiles. Eight Vulcan B2s took part, four each from No's 27 and 83 Squadrons, the former to attack from Kindley Air Force Base, Bermuda, and the latter flying from Lossiemouth, Scotland.

North and South waves attacked on 14 October, the Vulcans preceded by USAF B-47 Stratojets and B-52 Stratofortresses, with Martin RB-57s making spoof ECM attacks. Fighter defences against the northern wave concentrated on the B-47s and B-52s, and by the time the Vulcans entered North American airspace at 56,000ft the fighters didn't have the fuel to climb and intercept them. All four aircraft came through, landing at Stephenville, Newfoundland. It was a similar success for the southern wave. The Vulcans attacked on a broad front, then one turned away north while the other three shielded it with a jamming screen. The lone aircraft landed undetected at Plattsburgh AFB, New York, and whilst the other three all reported intercepts they were able to evade the fighters and get away, outflying the 'enemy' in single combat by applying full power and making a tight spiral turn upwards. Full details of Skyshield remained classified until 1997, American newsreels of the time reporting the defensive operations as "nearly 100% successful." The truth was a little different!

Skyshield provided the inspiration for a novel, The Penetrators (1965), but the reality was it didn't really reflect the Vulcan's role in the overall war plan of the time, where the aircraft wouldn't have the advantage of a fleet of USAF bombers running interference.

The target approach at the time, with the force carrying free-fall nuclear weapons, was to attack from altitude and make a tight 180 degree turn after releasing the bomb, to avoid the effects of the blast. Soviet missile defences were developing rapidly though, as demonstrated on 1 May 1960 when a American U-2 spyplane was shot down over the USSR whilst at 60,000ft. A complete change in the role of the V-Bomber therefore came about over the next few years, as it had become clear that in the absence of a long-range stand-off weapon, any attack, if it were to succeed, would have to be at low level under the radar. V-Bombers began to appear in a camouflage paint scheme appropriate to this new mission profile, replacing the all-white finish, and from 1966 were gradually equipped with Terrain Following Radar (TFR) mounted in a 'thimble' on the nose tip.

The change to low-level operations required Vulcan crews to undergo major changes in training, and the main responsibility for this fell to the Bomber Command detachment at Goose Bay in Labrador, Canada. The location had the advantages of a large areas of unpopulated terrain similar to the Arctic regions of the Soviet Union, and a lack of air traffic, and Vulcans visited every week of the year to fly low-level routes.

The final production B2, XM657, arrived at 35 Squadron in January 1965, and around the same time the Coningsby Wing (IX, 12 and 35 Squadrons) relocated to RAF Cottesmore in Rutland. At the end of 1967 12

Opposite page: On final approach at Scampton a Vulcan flies over the landing lights. *Terry Senior*

Below left: Blue Steel assembly line in 1959. *Verdon-Roe*

Below: The view from the cockpit as a Vulcan lines up on a Valiant tanker in 1961. *Richard Lewis*

Squadron was disbanded, its aircraft going to the Waddington Wing, and in April 1968 Bomber and Fighter Commands merged into Strike Command, the Vulcans maintaining the QRA vanguard for another year until strategic nuclear deterrent duties were handed over to the Royal Navy and Polaris in June 1969.

230 OCU moved from Finningley to Scampton towards the end of 1969. The Scampton Vulcans equipped to carry Blue Steel were converted to the free fall bomber role and this surplus of aircraft was soon found to be useful, as Vulcans were deployed to Cyprus to help strengthen the Central Treaty Organisation (CENTO). Nos IX and 35 Squadrons moved from Cottesmore to the warmer climate of RAF Akrotiri to form the Near East Air Force (NEAF) Bomber Wing, the squadrons vacating Cottesmore completely by March 1969. With the disbanding of 83 Squadron at the end of August 1969 seven Vulcan units remained (plus the OCU), three at Waddington, two at Scampton and two at Akrotiri, all now tasked with the conventional bombing role with free-fall weapons. Training priority was given to night operations to give a greater chance of survival in hostile environments, and major overseas trips continued.

Vulcans of 27 Squadron taxi out for a last flypast before being disbanded at Scampton. *Terry Senior*

On 29 March 1972, 27 Squadron disbanded at Scampton but re-formed on 1 November 1973 with Vulcans modified for the maritime strategic reconnaissance role, the aircraft being known as B Mk.2 MRR. The MRR Vulcans had Loran C navigation equipment, various electronic sensors, and photographic equipment fitted in the bomb-aimer's window. Some aircraft also carried air sampling pods on under-wing pylons in their secondary role of upper air sampling. A small change to the Vulcan's outline also arrived at this time, as the tailfin sprouted a rectangular fairing housing the antenna for the Marconi 18228 radar warning receiver. This improved on its predecessor by being able to display data on several threats at once.

The Turkish invasion of northern Cyprus in mid-1974 led to the Akrotiri Wing being dispersed to Malta before it was withdrawn from the Mediterranean altogether to help defuse the political situation. IX Squadron returned to Britain and joined the Waddington Wing, whilst 35 Squadron went to Scampton.

VULCAN MEMORIES

Crew Chief Chf Tech Bill Pearsey poses next to Avro Vulcan B2 XH562 of the NEAF Bomber (Akrotiri) Wing at RAF Masirah in March 1972. 562 was returning from a trip to New Zealand where it had been most spectacularly 'zapped' by personnel of the RNZAF. The squadron badge on the nose wheel door is that of No 75 Squadron RNZAF. Bill Pearsey remembers:

"The 'vandalism' was done at Ohakea. Even the station commander was involved. We threatened to fly under Sydney Harbour Bridge on the way back. We had arrived at Ohakea on the Monday; the following day we were taken on a trip to Roturua in a VIP Dakota. They were just removing the steps that they used to paint the kiwi as we arrived back in the evening. On the Wednesday we flew down to Christchurch. Some Yanks came to ask us how long us Kiwis had been operating Vulcans and my mate told them that 562 was the first of 94 that we were getting. Some months after I arrived back in Akrotiri I received a very large envelope containing a photo of a squadron of 9 Kiwi Vulcans flying over Ohakea control tower. It was definitely the best trip I ever did."

Flying the Vulcan during the Cold War
Martin Withers

In 2008, during one of her campaign speeches, I heard Hilary Clinton state quite simply about her defence policy, that if Iran were to launch a nuclear attack on Israel or any other country, "we would obliterate them". This is the language of the Cold War. USSR v USA (NATO) - a contest which neither side could win, because each knew that the other would retaliate against any nuclear attack with enough force to destroy the other.

Once or twice and particularly during the 'Cuban Missile Crisis' in 1962, we came dangerously close to mutual destruction. Vulcan crews were dispersed around the country and at cockpit readiness, armed with nuclear bombs and ready to launch. They were never 'scrambled', nevertheless, many crews spent long periods around that time on Quick Reaction Alert (QRA), and the possibility of a nuclear holocaust was very real. While the V-Force, from its inception, represented Britain's nuclear deterrent, gradually the only V-bomber remaining was the Vulcan. The Valiant had a short service life and the Victor was not strong enough to adapt from a high-level to the low level role necessitated by the development of Soviet missile systems. However by this time, we required fewer bombers because our primary nuclear weapons were the submarine launched Polaris missiles.

XL380 taxis out on a Lincolnshire morning.
Terry Senior

This was the state of play when I joined 44 Squadron at RAF Waddington in 1971. There were only 3 Vulcan bases remaining, Waddington, Scampton and Akrotiri (Cyprus), and a total of 7 squadrons plus the OCU. Each squadron would normally have 10 crews, and with 5 men on each crew, this represented some 350 V-Force aircrew around at any one time. It is no wonder that we never got to know everyone on the force. But there were always plenty of people in the bar on a Friday night and always enough for a party to celebrate any occasion.

Life at Waddington when I arrived there was sweet. There was plenty of friendly rivalry between the squadrons, we worked mainly between Monday and Friday, unless we were making trips abroad to Canada (Goose Bay), the USA (normally Offutt, the home of SAC HQ and the B-52), or Cyprus (before the partition and the influx of package holidays). We only had a training role, so did not fly more than about once a week, interspersed with the odd simulator trip, war target study and other ground training exercises. From time to time we would exercise our war role, particularly on NATO Tactical Evaluation Exercises (TACEVALS)

Looking back on those days life really was not hard!

XM647 whilst with 50
Squadron. *Terry Senior*

To many people it must be difficult to appreciate what it was like to fly a bomber which was without doubt a 'weapon of mass destruction'. I never knew of anyone who had any sleepless nights worrying about the prospect of dropping a 'nuke'. Quite simply, we trained hard to demonstrate to everyone that we had the skill, the knowledge and the determination to fly the Vulcan in all weathers, at low-level, day or night, avoiding Soviet defences and deliver a nuclear bomb with sufficient accuracy to destroy our target (usually one of military significance). By demonstrating this to the satisfaction of our lords and masters in the RAF, the rest of the Defence Staff and to our NATO chiefs (who valued the Vulcan highly as a 'second strike weapon'), we knew that we were part of an effective deterrent. We did not have to go to war to earn our keep.

If, however, Britain had come under nuclear attack from the USSR, I am convinced that we would have launched with absolute determination to hit our assigned targets with very little concern for our own safety, or for the devastating effects of our weapons. We would be aware that the deterrent role had failed, and that everything and everyone we cared about at home was very probably being destroyed as we pressed on to the target. But fortunately, nothing like that happened. We concentrated on our careers and secondary duties, enjoyed the 'lone rangers' abroad, the social life on the squadron, (greatly enhanced by the 'crew' concept, which meant that each crew remained together for most of the 2-3 year tour and therefore wives and partners all knew one another extremely well), and of course, we all loved the Vulcan!

I continued to fly the Vulcan as a captain on 50 Squadron also at Waddington, which was when I learnt that the captain not only has to take the blame when things go wrong, but also gets the praise when everything is going along well. But what we achieved was very much a crew effort at all times. By 1980, I was a QFI and was posted back to the Conversion Unit (230 OCU) as an instructor, but the OCU closed soon afterwards as the squadrons were about to disband and I moved back to Waddington, as the Squadron QFI/ Pilot Leader on 101 Squadron. By this time, I was quite impressed with the way the aircraft was being flown. We were flying down valleys and hiding behind hills rather than maintaining straight lines over ridges (in order to reduce fatigue) as I had been used to four years earlier.

We were also allowed to take part in Red Flag in the Nevada desert. It was all very encouraging, there was no intention of lowering standards because the Vulcan was going out of service. We were still assigned to NATO, and we were going out on a 'high' at the peak of our tactical effectiveness, yet we were being replaced by an aircraft without the range to take on our targets (Tornado). And then, the Vulcan was called upon to do her bit in the Falklands, and my crew having been selected as the reserve on 'Black Buck 1', ended up going all the way.

Winding down

Vulcan units had participated in the US based international exercise 'Giant Voice' for several years with good results. 1974's competition, held at Barksdale AFB, Louisiana, was the most successful and marked the first time an RAF crew won the Mathis Trophy for best crew in bombing and celestial navigation. Strike Command held its own version 'Double Top' in the UK, to which Strategic Air Command's B-52s were invited.

Competitions like these were good for morale, but weren't a good representation of actual combat, so in 1977 Strike Command jumped at the offer to participate in 'Red Flag'. These were realistic air warfare exercises held over the Arizona desert, designed to pit different aircraft types both against each other and against simulated Soviet ground defences. Operating from Nellis AFB, the Vulcan missions were aimed at penetrating a ring of ground-to-air defences, including dropping live 1,000lb bombs.

By the decade's end the fleet was nearing the end of operational service, with the Panavia Tornado due to replace both the Vulcan and Blackburn Buccaneer. In December 1980, the first aircraft to be scrapped, XM653, made its last flight to St Athan. With the need for conversion training at an end, 230 OCU was disbanded in mid-1981, followed by 617 Squadron in January 1982, the remaining two Scampton squadrons, 35 and 27, following in March.

Then came the unanticipated event that heralded the only time the Vulcan was used in anger, the invasion of the Falkland Islands in April 1982. The aircraft was the only type on the RAF's inventory capable of carrying a large bomb load over long range; even so, it would not be able to reach the Falklands. Flight-refuelling capability had to be restored, and crews re-trained in its use. Several aircraft underwent this and other hasty modifications, including the addition of Carousel Inertial Navigation, Shrike missiles and a Westinghouse ECM jamming pod on under-wing pylons (using the Skybolt mounting points). The undersides of the chosen aircraft were painted dark sea grey, and the squadron badges overpainted.

VULCAN MEMORIES

Alan Young, Flt Lt RAF Ret'd

I joined my first Vulcan Crew as AEO in 1966. Ten years later I was on a 50 Squadron display crew based at Waddington. That was the year of the US bi-centennial celebrations. It was agreed that the Lincoln copy of the Magna Carta would be shipped to the States to be displayed in San Francisco Cathedral as part of the celebrations.

The original plan was for it to be flown by civil airlines. The Dean was concerned about its security in transit particularly with the number of people who would need to be made aware of the travel arrangements both in the UK and the US. These included Police, Airport Security staff and baggage handlers and several aircrews to list but a few.

In the end, a special fire and water-proof box was constructed to contain this valuable cargo and as my crew, captained by Squadron Leader John Prideaux, was programmed to display at the Castle AFB open day in California, it was decided that the box containing the Magna Carta would be taken by us. This had the advantage of cutting the numbers of those who 'needed to know' about the move from several hundreds to a mere dozen or so.

On 29th September 1976, an armed convoy arrived at our aircraft (XM651). 'The box' was secured in the bomb-aimer's compartment with the co-pilot and I each being presented with a key to one of the two securing locks. Five hours later we arrived a Goose Bay and had to remain in the aircraft until it had been moved into a hangar which was then locked and guarded by RCMP for the next eight hours. Our seven man crew, including two crew chiefs, guarded the aircraft in pairs overnight.

The following day, after a six hour flight, we arrived at Castle AFB, to be surrounded by about 20 heavily armed USAF Military Police. A few minutes later the Deans of Lincoln and San Francisco Cathedrals and two armoured security vans arrived to take control of 'the box' for its transfer to San Francisco.

We seven crew members were each presented with an engraved cut-glass crystal goblet commemorating this historic occasion. Several months later another Vulcan crew flew the Magna Carta back to Waddington, that crew each also receiving a commemorative goblet.

Black Buck
Barry Masefield

It was 04.30 hours on 2 April 1982, when 150 men of the Argentine Special Forces landed by helicopter at Mullet Creek, a small inlet some three miles to the south-west of the Falklands' capital, Port Stanley. This was the beginning of the Argentinian take-over of the Falkland Islands, an event which was to rock the British government to its heels. Its response was to dispatch a Royal Naval Task Force accompanied by the Parachute Regiment southwards to capture the Falklands Islands. Back home, preparations were being made to involve the Royal Air Force Strike Command Vulcan fleet in the hostilities that were to come.

I was an AEO (Air Electronics Officer) on 50 Squadron at RAF Waddington. Three crews (plus one reserve) were to be selected for specialist training in air-to-air refuelling techniques, something which hadn't been done for some number of years, and also to carry out low-level 1,000lb live bomb attacks by day and night against targets in the north and west of Scotland in preparation for operations against as yet unknown targets in the South Atlantic. To assist us with the refuelling techniques we had assigned to each crew an AARI (Air-Air Refuelling Instructor) from the Victor OCU at RAF Marham.

Training began in earnest on 14 April with our first flight refuelling sortie which was fairly alarming to say the least. The AARI had to adjust to the sleek aerodynamic qualities of the Vulcan and to try and position the aircraft astern of the Victor tanker with the correct closing speed without overshooting the refuelling hose. To see the Victor up ahead closing rapidly was an experience and several times we sped past underneath it. However, it wasn't long before the pilots came to grips with the situation and good progress was made in training the Vulcan pilots in the skills of in-flight refuelling.

The main problem emerging now was that the seals in the refuelling probes were not performing correctly. Fuel spillage from the refuelling hose was covering the cockpit windows reducing visibility to virtually zero and, of equal concern, the fumes from the fuel were also entering the cockpit causing great anxiety about a potential fire. Modifications were carried out and new seals were fitted which helped reduce the problem, but supplies of seals were running out and a world-wide search was made to scavenge refuelling probes still fitted to Vulcans acting as gate guards and museum exhibits.

Training at the electronic warfare range at Spadeadam was introduced for the AEO. The anticipated Argentine radar systems had been programmed into the Spadeadam emitters and we flew evasive and jamming sorties against them whilst enroute to the bombing ranges. A new jammer equipment unit, the Westinghouse

Above: Barry on board XH558 whilst with the VDF. *Charles Toop*

Below: A Black Buck Vulcan taxis out at RAF Waddington. *Terry Senior*

ALQ101 pod, then currently fitted and in use on the Buccaneer fleet, was fitted to the underside of the wing, and the training continued by day and night using the Terrain Following Radar at very low level until the pilots became totally confident with the system and their ability. All the training was coming together, the ultra low-level flying using the TFR, the in-flight refuelling, the 1,000lb bombing, and the EW training at Spadeadam. The final target in the South Atlantic was still unknown and rumours were rife with Buenos Aires being the number one guess, but no one really knew; and Port Stanley airfield certainly hadn't ever been mentioned.

On 27 April, only two weeks from the start of the training, we were all gathered into the briefing room and told that the following day we would be flying south to Wideawake airfield on Ascension Island to prepare for a bombing raid on Port Stanley airfield on the night of 30 April. Squadron Leader John Reeves' crew was chosen to be the primary crew to carry out the mission with Flight Lieutenant Martin Withers' crew acting as our reserve. We were on our way, with our target known only to us and, of course, classified as Top Secret.

Our mission was to put the runway at Port Stanley airfield out of action to Argentine fighter aircraft, by landing at least one bomb on the runway. The Chief of the Air Staff had that morning been with the Prime Minister, Margaret Thatcher, who told him that not only was the mission of military importance it was also to be a political statement to the Argentinians that we could attack their homeland if necessary. To this end the crews were to be kept from any danger if possible during the mission! To achieve this we had to remain outside the range of any of the Argentine ground-air fire, which meant that we would have to fly at medium height around 10,000 feet whilst bombing the target.

So much for all the intensive low-level training we had been practicing in the previous weeks!

We arrived at Wideawake airfield on Ascension Island with the bombing mission planned for the following night, 30 April. The mission take-off was to be just before midnight with the pre-flight briefing to take place several hours beforehand. Not much sleep was had during that day as most of us were pumping sufficient adrenalin around our bodies to last a lifetime. The Vulcan crews gathered for their own private briefing by

the unit intelligence officer and by the SAS who gave us details about code words and 'safe houses' to make for should we be shot down. Soon it was time for the combined Victor and Vulcan briefing. This took place in a very large marquee with very poor acoustics and so the briefing was carried out by the briefing officer using a bull horn which I'm sure the whole of the island could hear and probably any spy trawler off shore!

The mission involved the use of 11 Victors and 2 Vulcans and used one of the most complex, refuelling plans ever devised. The briefing over, we proceeded to our respective aircraft, confident but nerves still jangling and the adrenalin still pumping. However, once inside the aircraft, we were so busy that soon the nerves were calmed and we treated it just like any other sortie and got on with the job. All was going well; the pre-taxi checks were carried out, but as the captain went to close his DV window he noticed that one of the seals had split. This potentially could be a major problem, but he elected to carry on anyway and hope that once airborne the seal would reseat itself and allow the aircraft to pressurise. It wasn't to be and after many attempts to try stuffing his flying jacket in the leak it soon became apparent that our aircraft was going nowhere that night. A radio call was made to Martin Withers to let him know of the situation and that he was now the primary bomber. I hear that it went a bit quiet on his aircraft for a while, but being the professionals they were, Martin just said 'It looks like we've got a job of work to do' and they proceeded southwards to complete their mission.

Our turn was to come a few days later on 3 May when, once again, we were chosen as the primary crew to carry out the next bombing mission on the same target. Now that the element of surprise that we could attack so far south had been lost, it was vital that communications between the aircraft were once again kept to an absolute minimum to avoid alerting the Argentinians that we were coming. This time all the aircraft got airborne successfully in absolute radio silence and we were on our way. During the briefing I noticed that our routing was to take us very close to the Task Force and that was of major concern to me. Having spent seventeen years working with the Royal Navy I was only too aware that in times of tension it was the Navy's policy that if any unidentified aircraft came within their missile engagement zone they would shoot first and ask questions afterwards. My attempts to find out whether the Task Force knew that we were coming were unsuccessful, and so we got airborne still not knowing, but desperately hoping that they were aware. Our flight south continued with no real problems except for some turbulence during the refuelling from the Victors.

At a point some two hundred miles short of the Falkland Islands we descended to ultra low level for the start of our run in over the sea to the target area. Already I could hear on my radar warning receiver the search radars from our navy ships looking for possible enemy aircraft, but we had no option but to continue our path towards them. Using my radar warning receiver, I could give bearings of the various radars to the navigator and by using three separate bearing lines he was able to plot a rough position of the ship. It was rough and ready, but the best we could do in the circumstances, our radar of course, was switched to standby to avoid alerting the enemy, so we couldn't use it to plot our ships. We continued to weave our way through the fleet emerging unscathed and at a point approximately twenty miles from the target we climbed to sixteen thousand feet for our run in to the target. The enemy radars seemed to be switched off until shortly before the final run in, when I could hear the airfield search radar switch on. I had already made a decision that provided only the airfield search radar was being used I would not jam it, as it was no threat to us and using my jammer would have acted like a beacon indicating our direction of approach. Only if the radars from the guns and missiles were heard would I start jamming, but there was no sign of them being used to locate us.

At the appropriate range, the bomb doors were opened and the bombs dropped. I made an attempt to count the explosions but it was virtually impossible to hear anything above the roar of the Olympus engines as they were put to full throttle to enable us to climb up to high level turning northwards. The Nav. Radar switched on his radar to sector scan the Task Force, as this was pre-arranged so that they would know we had completed our bombing raid and were on our way home. My radar warning receiver then went into overload from all the gun and missile radars being directed towards us from the ships. Fortunately we were well outside their armament range and so they presented no threat to us.

I transmitted the codeword 'Superfuse' on the HF radio back to base to let them know we had dropped the bombs, were on our way home, and would be requiring a Victor to top us up. The journey northward off the coast of Argentina was not without incident. For some unknown reason, there was heavy electrical interference which occasionally manifested itself by giving indications on the radar warning receiver that we had a fighter on our tail. I don't think I've seen knuckles quite so white as those of the Navs each time the RWR lit up. Using the periscope and the tail warning receiver, it became apparent after several scares that it was just electrical interference and was nothing to worry about.

We eventually spotted the Nimrod which was on patrol waiting to escort us back to Ascension Island. Soon after that, the most welcome sight of our Victor tanker hove into view and he successfully topped us up with sufficient fuel to get us home. We landed 14 hours 45 minutes after take-off feeling quite elated that we had done the job we had been tasked with. Shortly after the de-brief, we retired to the bar for a few well earned beers and a decent night's sleep. There were several more sorties involving the Vulcan aircraft using air/ground missiles against the Argentinians and also further bombing missions; all full of incident, but that's another story.

Below: Black Buck Vulcan XM597, with XH560 in the foreground. *Terry Senior*

A last hurrah

The Falklands had other consequences for the Vulcan that were to extend its service career a little longer. Operations in the South Atlantic had diverted a large proportion of the Victor tanker fleet, not just the eleven per sortie needed for each Black Buck mission, but additional aircraft to refuel Nimrod and Hercules operations. The fleet's remaining fatigue life was being rapidly consumed, and although the RAF had purchased Vickers VC10 airliners from British Airways to convert to a transport and tanker role, these would not be completed for some time yet.

This left only one option, and six Vulcans from 50 Squadron were chosen for tanker conversion, known as Modification 2600. Hose-and-drogue units (borrowed from the VC10 programme) would be installed in the tail, replacing the ECM cans. Lack of space meant the units had to be partially contained in ungainly wooden fairings that became known variously as the dog-box, kennel or skip! Three cylindrical fuel tanks were fitted in the bomb-bay, with control of the pumps being via a panel added to the retractable fuel control console in the cockpit. The nav radar's panel had indicators and switches installed for the HDU bay heating and bomb-bay temperature, while the nav plotter's panel gained panels for lighting control, HDU monitoring and a press-to-transmit switch for contacting the aircraft requiring refuelling. To assist in guiding refuelling aircraft the Vulcan's undersides were painted white towards the rear, with Day-Glo striping outlined in black also applied.

The first aircraft for conversion, XH561 arrived at Woodford on 4 May 1982 and rolled out for its first flight on 18 June. The last of the six, XH558 was completed on 3 September. Alongside these, designated K2, 50 Squadron also operated three standard B2s for continuation training and aircrew qualification tasks.

By the end of the year the squadron was the last RAF Vulcan unit. 101 Squadron had been disbanded in August followed by 44 Squadron on 21 December. As each VC10 reached the point of requiring its HDU, so the Vulcan tankers were withdrawn one by one, until 50 Squadron was finally disbanded on 31 March 1984.

Above: Three bomb-bay tanks.

Below: Three 50 Squadron tankers, with standard B2 XL426 to the left.
Terry Senior

Above: XH560 with refuelling drogue deployed. *MoD/Crown Copyright*

This photo: Closeup on XH558's tail, showing the 'dog-box'. *Terry Senior*

This was still not the end of service though. Two aircraft, XL426 and XH558, were to be retained for display purposes, operated by the Vulcan Display Team, which came under 55 Squadron, a Victor tanker unit based at Marham. On 30 November 1984 XH558 was flown to Waddington to be returned to B2 standard, or at least as close as could be achieved. With the HDU removed the rear fuselage was basically an empty shell, affecting the aircraft's centre of gravity. To compensate, a cylindrical fuel tank was fitted in the rear position and XH558 then flew to Kinloss to be repainted in a high-gloss wraparound camouflage scheme.

XL426 was running out of hours and was put up for sale, leaving XH558 in 1986 as the sole Vulcan in RAF service. That came to an end in 1993 when the aircraft was sold to C Walton Ltd at Bruntingthorpe, and the delivery flight on 23 March marked the end of the Avro Vulcan's RAF career, 37 years after the first B1 entered service.

The Vulcan story however, was not yet quite over...

XH558 in 1992, her last display season with the RAF. *Charles Toop*

The First - VX770

Avro 698 prototype VX770 made its maiden flight on 30 August 1952, powered by Rolls-Royce Avon RA. 3 engines of 6,500lb thrust. Finished in gleaming white, it wore the Avro badge, RAF roundels and fin flashes and was piloted by chief test pilot Roly Falk, immaculately dressed as ever. At this point the aircraft had only minimum systems, so Falk flew solo.

Following appearances in the air at the SBAC show in September VX770 returned to the hangar for further work, including fitting modified pilots' panels, air-conditioning and pressurization systems and the co-pilot ejector seat. Test flying resumed at the end of October, with 32 hours logged by late January 1953. In May 1953, VX770 was fitted with 7,500lb thrust Armstrong Siddeley Sapphire turbojets for high-speed high-altitude trials, and wing fuel tank balancing systems to allow the centre of gravity to be maintained automatically. Flight trials with Avro and A&AEE crews, plus an RAF liaison team, kept VX770 busy through 1955 and up to June 1956 when the aircraft began trials with Rolls-Royce Conway engines.

The more powerful engines allowed the aircraft to fly higher and faster than before, and it was at this point the Avro team found the severe buffeting that had affected the Type 707A at high speeds and altitudes also occurred in the Vulcan. The Phase 2 wing modification was designed to overcome this, but before VX770 could benefit it was destroyed during a display at RAF Syerston on 20 September 1958. The aircraft was being flown by a three-man Rolls-Royce crew, captained by test pilot K. Sturt, who had over 1,600 flying hours, 91 of them on VX770, and was judged to be a 'capable and careful pilot'. As the aircraft made a fast flypast the starboard wing leading edge stripped away and the wing structure collapsed. In the crash that followed the port wing destroyed the fire/rescue Land Rover and runway controller's caravan, killing three ground crew and injuring a fourth. All four members of the Vulcan crew were killed. From the first indication of structural failure to the time of the crash was approximately 6 seconds.

VX770 in flight.
Cyril Peckham

Taking off on her maiden flight at Woodford.

Subsequent investigation suggested the pilot had been flying lower and faster than authorised, 400 knots according to one eyewitness, though experienced Vulcan test pilot Tony Blackman concluded this was unlikely as he knew the pilot in question and didn't believe he would have been reckless enough to ignore the briefed flypast speed of 300 knots. Blackman pointed out that, as the prototype, VX770 was not as strong as a production Mk.1: "At Woodford we had a special small man in the ground crew who could and would climb up and inspect inside the leading edges for damage, because sometimes the nose ribs buckled and had to be repaired. As far as I know Rolls-Royce knew nothing of these inspections and they may not have been looking at the leading edges internally between every flight."

Whatever the cause, the tragedy brought to an end the life of the first Vulcan after just six years.

VX770s wing collapses in mid-air at Syerston, 1958.

First Flight of Vulcan Prototype VX770 in 1952 remembered...

Sue Kennett (daughter of Avro Chief Designer, Stuart Davies)

August 30th 1952, a Saturday I believe. A beautiful summers day and we assembled in front of the Club House at Woodford to watch this historic event - namely, the first flight of 698 as she was called. She did look rather lovely as we waited for her to move.

Below: VX770 takes off on her maiden flight. *Sandy Jack*

Right: VX770 displaying with both rear undercarriage doors removed.

Roly Falk started off down the runway on what I, at nearly 13 years old, thought was the take off, but he was teasing us and just doing a test taxi run. Anyway, shortly afterwards, she lifted off and started doing the thing at which she excelled - showing her paces. Everyone was chatting about how well that part had gone but my father, a man of few words on this sort of occasion, enquired what else would be expected, as the 707s had been busy for several years testing the delta shape on a much smaller scale. After, perhaps, 30 minutes, the plane returned but I seem to recall that something fell off! Was it a cover to the undercarriage? I feel sure there is a more technical term!

Anyway, a couple of planes, one a 707, I seem to remember* flew up to check everything was OK and it was decided that the wheels were locked down and all would be well. My father continued to be upbeat about this small incident on the basis that the plane was not flying very fast! The 698, soon to be known as the Vulcan, landed perfectly with the parachute streaming out behind her and slowed to a halt whilst the assembled audience clapped.

Roly Falk reported that everything had gone very well. In those times of austerity (I think we still had food rationing) I seem to think that we had nothing much to celebrate with other than tea and biscuits. Several days later, at the Farnborough Air Show, Roly Falk again demonstrated the white 698 with a red 707 on one side and a blue one on the other. I recall that the spectators at the show rose to their feet in applause.

*The 707A was flown by Jimmy Nelson, who had already flown that day and was low on fuel on the ground, so made a hasty take-off to help check over the aircraft, but landed as soon as the other aircraft, a de Havilland Vampire, was airborne. No damage was found and the aircraft landed without further incident. The Vampire was piloted by Jack Wales.

Brake parachute deployed
at Farnborough, 1953.
Barry Jones

Peter Caldwell (Avro employee)

The production of the Type 698 continued apace. The fuselage had arrived in the Flight Sheds and the first prototype, VX770 was ready for flight by August 1952. Among the many pre-flight tests, we played our part with the fuel system which for the initial flight was only using the long range bomb-bay tanks. It must be shown that it is possible to deliver 1.25 times the maximum take-off flow rate to each engine with a fuel pressure of at least 5 p.s.i. at the engine inlet in all configurations of direct and cross feeding. Engines were simulated by pumps passing fuel through a type of flow-meter. When the full fuel system was subsequently used and tested by our department the initial tests took four days and nights without a break, testing in all possible configurations of direct and cross feeding. We took it in turns to go home for a few hours.

The day arrived for the initial flight which was planned for the evening and most of us stayed behind to watch the momentous event. The large white aircraft with its futuristic shape stood on the apron in all its glory and the chief test pilot, Roly Falk, sat in an Armstrong Siddeley car, with whose makers Avro were then associated, waiting for the finishing touches to be completed. He was accompanied by one of the directors and I recall that both men wore pin-striped suits which turned out to be the standard attire of this Chief Test Pilot in addition to his helmet. Other dignitaries were there, including Sir Roy Dobson, the Managing Director. Eventually, Roly donned his helmet and boarded the aircraft. Engines were started and away he taxied. To our disappointment, all we were treated to was a couple of fast taxies before dusk turned to dark, and we all went home.

The following day being Saturday, I decided to go in, but instead of going across to the Flight Sheds, I sat on an old air-raid shelter which gave me a pretty good view of the runway. I saw the aircraft come onto the runway, and gain speed for what I was sure would be another fast taxi, but instead it gained momentum and soared into the air in a graceful climb circling the aerodrome at about 3000 ft accompanied by a small chase aircraft, the make of which I have forgotten. After a few circuits, unlike most maiden flights on which a new design ventured away from the base to commence its test programme, the wheels were dropped and a small piece of material was seen to flutter to the ground before VX770 made a perfect landing to commence a useful career. The piece that fell was a rear undercarriage door flap which did not interfere with flight, and I believe that for its subsequent appearance at Farnborough 1952 they removed the equivalent part on the other side for the sake of symmetry when viewed and photographed from the ground.

The Last - XH558

Above: Photographed during an early test flight prior to entering service with the RAF. *Rolls-Royce*

Below: In MRR role with 27 Squadron, air sampling pods clearly visible under the wing. *Terry Senior*

Avro Vulcan serial number XH558 was ordered under a MoD contract placed in September 1954. XH558 was completed at Avro's Woodford factory in 1960 and was first flown on 25 May that year. The aircraft was finally completed on 30 June and on the 1 July XH558 became the first Vulcan B Mk.2 to enter RAF service at RAF Waddington.

XH558 then moved to RAF Finningley in 1961, serving with No 230 operational conversion unit (OCU) training Vulcan Pilots for Squadron service. Between 1968 and August 1973 the aircraft served with Nos 44, 50 and 101 Squadrons at RAF Waddington. In August 1973 the aircraft was converted to maritime radar reconnaissance (MRR) standard, remaining in this role with No 27 Squadron at RAF Scampton until March 1982 when she was returned to Waddington and No 44 Squadron.

With the outbreak of the Falklands conflict in April 1982, XH558 was converted again, this time to a stop-gap tanker role, known as the K2 version. Although XH558 took no further part in the conflict, her current Chief Display Pilot is ex Squadron Leader Martin Withers DFC, who flew the Vulcan that carried out the first Black Buck bombing raid on Port Stanley airfield during the conflict.

By 1984 the Vulcan fleet had been retired from Royal Air Force service, the final official RAF sortie being on the 26 March 1984 when XH560 carried out a refuelling mission. XH558 was flown to RAF Marham on the 17 September 1984 to see out her final days on the fire dump there. Two aircraft were

to be kept in service for public displays; Avro Vulcan XL426 continued on the Vulcan Display Team, and XH560 was initially chosen as the back up aircraft until it was found that XH558 had more flying hours remaining, and was rescued from the dump! XL426 gave her last display on the team in June 1986 and was then replaced by XH558, which had made her debut air display just a couple of weeks earlier at RAF Mildenhall on 24 May 1986.

XH558 remained with the now renamed Vulcan Display Flight until 20 September 1992 when she flew her final display in RAF hands at Cranfield's Dreamflight show. In February 1993 the MoD put XH558 up for auction with a view to her disposal as soon as possible, and with her subsequent sale to C. Walton Ltd the last Vulcan finally left the RAF. XH558 was thus the first B Mk.2 to enter service, and the last to leave, after a career of 33 years.

The aircraft was delivered by the RAF to Bruntingthorpe Aerodrome in Leicestershire on 23 March 1993. David Walton, Managing Director of C. Walton Ltd, had also purchased a huge stock of spares including eight Olympus 202 engines, with the thought that one day perhaps XH558 would fly again. With the support of retired RAF engineering officer Earl Pick and Peter Beushaw, the last Vulcan Chief Designer, David had discussed the possibility with the Civil Aviation Authority, but had been told that a "corporate response" was required. Other than a few fast taxi days, XH558 then sat at Bruntingthorpe.

In spring of 1997, Dr Robert Pleming, a career technical manager and Vulcan enthusiast, met David Walton, and asked for his agreement to tackle the issues raised by a return to flight. Pleming formed a small 'core team' to conduct a feasibility study into what was required. Included in the team were David Walton, Earl Pick and Peter

Above: XH558 undergoing maintenance whilst in K2 tanker guise. *MoD*

Below: Air-to-air in her last season with the VDF. *Charles Toop*

Beushaw but also XH558 aircrew David Thomas and Barry Masefield, Keith Mans, an ex-Vulcan pilot and Chief Executive of the Royal Aeronautical Society, and David Thorpe, XH558's last Crew Chief. In the same year Colin Mears established the XH558 Supporters Club, later to become the Vulcan to the Sky Club, a major source of funds and volunteers in the years to come.

The core team started to put together an audacious Return to Flight Project Plan; it was clear that the project, even if technically feasible, would be uniquely complex, challenging and expensive. Key to success was the regulatory requirement for the contractual support of British Aerospace as the successor organisation to Avro. By May of 1999, Pleming's project plan had acquired sufficient credibility to gain the support of British Aerospace. In the autumn of 1999, XH558 was pushed into the hangar at Bruntingthorpe for a technical survey, which showed that there were no fundamental show-stoppers to a return to flight.

Over 2000-2001, the core team confirmed the formal support of all the manufacturers needed for XH558's restoration, and reached agreement in principle from the CAA that XH558 could be restored to flight. With a budget estimate of £3.5million needed for the restoration, funding became the main challenge, so to complement the successful campaign run by Felicity Irwin, a £2.7million grant was sought from the Heritage Lottery Fund. As pre-requisite to a grant, the Vulcan to the Sky Trust, a charity, was formed in 2002 to own XH558 for the nation. News that the grant had been awarded in principle came through in December 2003.

Opposite: Air-to-air in 2011. *Tom Houquet/ aviation-photocrew.com*

Below: 18 October 2007, first flight. *Charles Toop*

Fundraising to top up the HLF grant continued through 2004; on 28 February 2005 VTTST purchased XH558 and all her spares and documentation, and on 28 April, the Trust and Marshall Aerospace Ltd (as the Engineering Authority) signed the contract that formalised the start of restoration work. The schedule of tasks included not only an extended Major service but also significant rectification work, overhaul of all operational systems and a modification of the rear spar to extend fatigue life (Mod 2222). In addition, a lot of non-essential equipment was to be removed. Five Marshall Aerospace technicians would be supported by up to 10 Vulcan to the Sky engineers, and a further 10 logistics and administration staff and some subcontractors. In addition, up to 20 design engineers at the Marshall Aerospace Design Office in Cambridge would be involved. In total, the project would need over 100,000 manhours of effort.

After being grounded for almost 14 years, Avro Vulcan XH558 finally took to the skies again on 18 October 2007. After first flight, XH558 returned to the airshow scene in July 2008. Now over 5 years since that first flight, and having entertained millions of people at airshows here and in Europe, the aircraft is looking forward to the 2013 airshow season, and is once again based at Finningley (now Robin Hood Airport Doncaster Sheffield).

Flying XH558 on the OCU
Peter Thomas

With the MkII ground and simulator course behind me I was now prepared and ready for my first flight. Significantly, it was in a brand new shiny white XH558 and on a brief systems test flight following its acceptance servicing. As it turned out that was not to be the end of my association and relationship with that very particular aircraft. For the 'train spotters' the OCU, at the time, had three other MkII's on strength and numbered; XH559, XH561 and XH562.

Before we could start using the aircraft for training the OCU and staff instructors were tasked with flying off 200 hours in order to establish future servicing and spares requirements. This meant flying around the clock 24 hours a day without respite. No sooner had the aircraft landed than it was serviced, refuelled and off again. We flew various navigation different profiles just to 'get the hours in'. Sometimes just a big, I mean big, square. I did a number of flights landing at Idris in Libya. Relations have indeed changed since those days. Idris was once called Castel Benito and was an ex Italian Air Force base.

It was great to get airborne with a 100% fuel load - set the cruise switch to cruise - open the throttles to the gate - wait until the climbing airspeed translated to cruising mach number and maintain that mach number. As the fuel load reduced so the aircraft would gradually climb. On one of these profiles I gave a courtesy call to Gibraltar ATC reporting overhead at Flight Level 500 and climbing. This was interpreted by the controller as 5,000 ft. and took a lot of convincing that we were in fact at 50,000ft. His laconic reply was; "no known traffic". Not surprising seeing as at that time it was the only aircraft capable and flying, apart from the U2 spy plane, at that sort of altitude! Later we were told not to report specific altitudes but simply say above Flight Level 400. For the early sixties this sort of performance was unknown. Later flights to the States utterly confused their controllers when they asked us to report on a climb out - let's say for instance - passing 4,000ft only to be told we are already through 14,000ft.

Extract from Squadron Leader Thomas' log book, showing the entry for his first flight with XH558 on 10 December 1960. His co-pilot, F/L Peter Douglas, was promoted to Squadron Leader the next day.

Barry Masefield *is the Air Electronics Officer (AEO) for Vulcan XH558 and has flown in this iconic aircraft for over 30 years, also being a key member of the Vulcan Display Flight (VDF), the RAF Unit which memorably flew the aircraft on the Airshow circuit until September 1992. Barry was also a member of the crew that flew XH558 into Bruntingthorpe Airfield on 23 March 1993 - her final flight in RAF service, and took part in the Black Buck missions in 1982.*

Along with Vulcan pilot David Thomas, Barry was part of the core team put together in 1997 to investigate the feasibility of restoring XH558, and on 18 October 2007, he was once again flying as part of the crew, alongside Al McDicken and David Thomas, who made the historic post-restoration First Flight from Bruntingthorpe. Barry has been a regular member of the Aircrew of XH558 since 2008, and has helped to thrill crowds around the country at Airshows and other events with a spectacular and memorable flying display, which has captured the hearts and minds of many thousands of spectators.

A full history of XH558's service career, restoration and return to flight can be found in our 50th anniversary book. These extracts from Barry's online blog bring the story up to date, covering the 2011-12 airshow seasons.

Ramblings From The AEO's Panel

The start of the 2011 display season was upon us and the aircrew stirred from their winter hibernation. In February we all gathered at our navigator Andy Marson's house for two days of refresher lectures on the aircraft systems, and the following Monday the AEOs went down to Hinckley to meet up with Taff Stone, our Crew Chief, to carry out our electrical circuit board training. It never ceases to surprise me that having flown the Vulcan for over 30 years, I still find something that I wasn't aware of and it confirms that flying 558 is a continual learning process.

Each year we have to renew our qualifications on emergency procedures and under the guidance of Andy, who's also our Flight Safety Officer, we carried out various drills on how to evacuate the aircraft under emergency conditions. The MaPS team at Wellesbourne Mountford kindly lent us their aircraft, XM655, for the day so that we could perform the drills under realistic conditions with the engines running. Running the aircraft and taxiing it for a short while gave our newer pilots the opportunity to keep their hands in and get used to the feel of 'driving' a Vulcan once again.

Now we had the emergency procedures sorted it was a case of waiting until 29 March, the date for us to fly 558 up to Robin Hood from her winter home at RAF Lyneham. For the military minded, Robin Hood Airport is the old RAF Finningley, a base that the Vulcan operated from for many years. The crew for the flight was Martin Withers, Paul Mulcahy (the CAA Chief Test Pilot), Andy Marson, as our Navigator, and myself. Although the aircraft didn't need to complete an air test after the winter servicing it would have to have one before July when the Permit To Fly was renewed, so this seemed an ideal opportunity to tick that box.

We got the distinct impression from all the Ops staff at Lyneham that they were all rather sad to see us go but they all knew, like we did, that staying at Lyneham was not an option seeing as it was due to close. We have received an excellent service from them and our thanks go to all of them for helping us. With pre-flight planning done we arrived at the aircraft, and soon we were roaring off down the runway for our flight to Doncaster. After a farewell flypast we turned eastwards to overfly Wootton Bassett at 2,000 feet to pay our respects to the townsfolk there. An overflight at RAF Brize Norton followed and then we continued our flight up to the RAF Marham area in East Anglia where we had our test flight schedule to carry out. This was done up at

14,000 feet and involved amongst many other things shutting down all the engines in turn, checking out the flying control systems and finally making sure that all the emergency electrical systems worked when electrical loads were placed on them. On arrival at Doncaster, Martin carried out a fly-through down the runway so that the crowds could see us before turning downwind for the landing. As part of the air test we had to stream the brake parachute, this always looks impressive and just enhanced our arrival.

After the aircraft was shut down we all stepped out to meet the airport dignitaries and a barrage of press photographers and TV crews. There seemed to be a genuine feeling of welcome from everyone who was there which bodes really well for our future operations from Robin Hood. Once all the hand shaking and pleasantries were over we carried out a comprehensive debrief with Taff about how the aircraft had performed. Overall, XH558 was in good condition and, after a period of minor rectification, was ready for our first display, the Abingdon air show on 8 May. Then, on 25 May, she took pride of place in her new home in hangar 3 at Robin Hood airport as the backdrop for a civic ceremony held by the 'great and the good' of Doncaster to welcome the Vulcan and the VTTST.

Above and below: XH558 arriving at Robin Hood Airport. *Andrew Brown and Lewis Steeper*

Then came a very busy weekend with an air show at Southend and a static display at Bruntingthorpe. After the display on the seafront, we flew the few miles north to Southend airport to overfly the Vulcan, XL426, based there. XL426 was our sister aircraft on the Vulcan Display Flight back in the '80s and she is lovingly being looked after by the enthusiasts down there in Essex.

We set course for Bruntingthorpe where XH558 was going to be used as a static aircraft at the Cold War Jets show the following day. I'm told that the gate numbers increased markedly once the public had been told that the Vulcan was going to be on the ground. We experienced that at first hand on the Sunday morning when trying to get into the airfield!

The day seemed to be a great success for David Walton, the owner of Bruntingthorpe and the original owner of XH558 after she was sold off by the MOD, and despite the weather being very windy and overcast the crowd thoroughly enjoyed watching all the various aircraft he has in his collection start up and fast taxi down the runway. We had a very enjoyable day in the VTTST tent, signing books and other paraphernalia and having a chance to meet up with our ever faithful public. We were the last event of the day and were programmed to take off at about 5.30pm.

Although all the museum aircraft had finished their taxiing displays sometime before, there was no sign of the crowd diminishing, none of them were about to leave knowing that the Vulcan was going to get airborne. The sortie was to be a re-introduction to the Vulcan for the newest of our pilot fraternity, Bill Ramsey. Bill is a very experienced display pilot having been the RAF Grob Tutor display pilot up until last year. He had previously been a Vulcan pilot years ago and had also been associated with the Red Arrows as their team manager.

On Friday 10 June, the aircraft went 'overseas' to display at the Isle of Man TT races venue. The week's racing was completed with an evening display by the Vulcan. From what I hear from those who were there, it was a very impressive display flown by Kevin Rumens with Bill Perrins as his co-pilot. Phil Davies was the AEO on that trip accompanied by Martin Andrews, our new AEO, for whom this was his first trip in a Vulcan. According to our ground crew, Martin was grinning like a Cheshire cat when he stepped off the aircraft and had thoroughly enjoyed the experience. His next flight was to scheduled to be with me a couple of days later for the RAF Cosford open day display, but the weather on that day was atrocious and well below our limits for flying. Consequently, we had no option but to cancel. As aircrew, we get very dejected when that happens, feeling disappointment for the many thousands of people who had spent their hard earned cash to watch us fly.

XH558 pictured air-to-air after departing the Abingdon airshow.
Tom Houquet/aviation-photocrew.com

It was to be another five days before 558 got airborne again when, on Friday 17 June, she completed her transit down to Kemble to be ready for her display the following day. Martin Andrews had his second trip that day and I'm told that his grin hadn't lessened when he stepped off the aircraft. The following day 558 successfully flew the Kemble and Margate displays with Phil Davies as the AEO.

Waddington was the next show and the transit flight was to be a successful final handling check for Bill Ramsey. This involved doing some aircraft handling with runway approaches and overshoots before finally touching down at Waddington. It was the Press day for the airshow and the TV and newspaper reporters were there to interview the crew. That weekend saw wonderful weather and enabled Waddington to provide the public with yet another unforgettable air show.

XH558 returns to Bruntingthorpe for Cold War Jets Day. *Charles Toop*

With RAF Waddington done and dusted it was time to organise 558's transit down to RN Yeovilton to be in position for their Open Day the following weekend of 9 July. The crew, comprising Martin Withers, Bill Ramsey and myself met up at Waddington Operations on the Tuesday morning, and as I made my way up the ladder into the cockpit, I was met by Martin Andrews (now nicknamed Junior) making his way down. He had been in the cockpit for about an hour practicing his skills using the Garmin GNS 430, the rear crew GPS system. One can only admire his devotion to duty!

As we progressed through the start-up checks all went well until we tried to start the third engine (No2), it just flatly refused to accelerate past the Idle power setting. We decided to dispense with the air starter unit and use the already started engines to supply compressed air to start up No2. Once again the engine turned but refused to accelerate past the Idle setting. Blast, we thought or words to that effect. We had no option now but to shut everything down and hand the aircraft back to Taff and his techies to sort out the problem.

Ray Watts, our engines techie, with the aid of Taff and the rest of the guys traced the problem to a faulty fuel bleed valve in the CMFS (Chassis Mounted Fuel System). This unit controls all the fuel requirements for the engine and after some adjustments, the guys came to the conclusion that there was no option but to change the entire CMFS. Not an easy thing to do, because normally the engine and the CMFS are changed together

as a complete unit when the engine is out of the aircraft, so getting to the fuel pipe joints is really difficult when the whole thing is still mounted in the wing. A replacement CMFS was transported up to Waddington, and as there was no chance that the engine was going to be fixed for a few days we aircrew packed our bags and returned home.

Eventually on Friday morning, Martin Withers rang us to say that things were progressing well and we returned to Waddington, where the techies were still working but felt confident that they would have the job wrapped up shortly. Finally, the call came that the engine had been declared serviceable and we made our way to the aircraft to be met by the techies. The poor guys looked absolutely shattered, they had worked extremely hard to get the engine serviceable and it had taken its toll. We climbed in and with Ray as our passenger for the trip we completed our checks. The transit went smoothly and all the engines behaved themselves so well done to all the techies who had put in so much hard work to achieve this.

Out with the old... VTTST engineers remove the CMFS on No. 2 engine. *Taff Stone*

Opposite: Displaying at Yeovilton and Fairford. *Barry Best and Michaela Park*

The display day at Yeovilton was yet another great success for the Vulcan. We had pre-briefed an add-on at the end of our display with the pilot of the RN Historic Flight Sea Vixen whereby when we had finished our display he would join up with us and we would fly past the crowds a few times to give them a unique photo opportunity. It all went well and the crowd loved it. After landing, we taxied the aircraft right up to the crowd line and after climbing out we were greeted with rapturous applause. Quite humbling really, but it's great to see how much the spectators love the aircraft and all that it stands for.

The aircraft was going to remain at Yeovilton for the rest of the week before it was then due to transit to Fairford for the Royal International Air Tattoo. I was due a bit of a break now, so RIAT had come and gone before I joined up with the crew and the aircraft again to re-position her at RAF Wittering for their Families Day on 22 July. The briefing done, we all arrived at the aircraft in good time for Jnr to do all his checks. This was to be his first complete sortie as the AEO and, needless to say, he was a bit nervous at first, but he coped admirably. Once we were airborne I asked him if he was ok and having received a nod, I left him to it and went up the ladder to look out between the pilots. The aircraft remained at Wittering for the next four days until the show, and considering that Wittering was in the throes of reducing its personnel, there was a great turnout.

As the following day dawned we were met with glorious sunshine, so the displays at both Southport and Windermere promised to be a photographers dream. We drove to the aircraft to be met by a rather large crowd of interested bystanders who were milling around the aircraft (I suspect Toni Hunter was running one of her much loved tours). This presented a small problem for me because, due to the fact that we had no power unit to give me power to the aircraft, I would have to use our own little on-board jet engine called the AAPP (Airborne Auxiliary Power Plant) to give me some AC power. In the starboard wing there is a downwards facing exhaust from the unit that blows out extremely hot gasses once running, and if any unsuspecting bystanders were to walk under it they would be in danger of getting quite badly singed. The crowds were dispersed by our ground crew so I could light up the AAPP and get our checks going. By this time, there was bit of cloud cover starting to build up so once airborne we could only climb up to about 2,000 feet for the transit. We had rather hoped to go a bit higher to cool down the aircraft ready for Martin to do his displays. One of the Achilles heels of the Vulcan, and it has several, is that the cooling system on the aircraft leaves a lot to be desired.

I noticed on a few of the wing-overs during the display that there was a large crowd gathered on the Southport sea front, and later heard from members of the public that they all thought the display put on that day was one of the best they had seen there. It was then time to input the GPS coordinates for the flight northwards to Windermere. On contacting the Display Director we found that the event was running behind schedule as

Over the hills (and spectators) at Windermere. *Tom Hill*

Above: Climbing over the Lake District hills. *Charles Toop*

Sequence above right: Removing and replacing the No. 2 fuel tank bladder. *Taff Stone*

Opposite: Spectacular scenery in the Lakes. *Neil Bury*

there was an incident in the vicinity which required the use of the Air Ambulance helicopter. Obviously, he took priority so the display was postponed until after he had landed.

Because we now had something like twenty minutes to kill, we climbed up to 3,000 feet and stooged around the Lake District to admire the beautiful scenery, and how beautiful it was. I've been to the Lake District on many occasions hill walking, but never have I seen the area look more beautiful than it was on that day. Eventually we got the call to say that we were cleared to carry out our display. This was the first time I had done this venue and I was quite excited to see how it would all look from my side windows with the mountains as a back-drop. I was not to be disappointed and the display flown by Martin was truly a wonderful experience. All too soon it was over and we departed for Doncaster. The weather was kind enough for us to climb up to 7,000 feet which cooled down the aircraft, and more importantly, the pilots who had been working extremely hard in a challenging display environment.

The next venue was the Sunderland seaside show, but after successfully flying there, XH558 went through a fairly torrid time. A few days before we were due to fly at the Bournemouth, Shoreham, Oxford and Dawlish displays, Taff and his team were fuelling the aircraft when they noticed a leak dripping from an area just aft of the nose-wheel doors. Refuelling was immediately stopped for investigations to be carried out. We have a total of fourteen fuel tanks, ten of which are in the wings, but the biggest four are in the main fuselage and positioned just above and aft of the nose wheel area. Unfortunately, the leak was in one of those very large tanks, No2 to be exact.

Having discovered the leak there was no option but for our engineers to drain the tank and inspect it to discover the source. As you can imagine, a tank that has recently been drained of its fuel is still full of very highly toxic and explosive vapour, so it had to be filled with compressed air to blow the vapour out. I'm not too sure of the safety distance around the aircraft when this procedure is being carried out but I'm sure that there was no-one having a crafty cigarette within a hundred yards. Once the tank had been made safe our techies could get inside it to inspect the inner bladder. They did indeed discover a few pin prick holes and so the bladder had to be taken out and sent to the manufacturer in Portsmouth for repair. Unfortunately, so I'm told, the factory personnel were all stood down on their summer holidays and wouldn't be back for a couple of weeks. It was obvious that we were not going to be able to fly the Bournemouth display weekend but we really would like to fly the following weekend at Dunsfold if at all possible, but it looked as if that was going to a pipe dream. However, our guardian angel came to the rescue yet again. The factory found some of their workers who

Philip Berry

were prepared to come in and work on the tank, and within a couple of days had got the thing repaired. To say 'thank you' to these guys is just simply inadequate, they ensured that potentially thousands of the public would get to see us again very soon, all due to their efforts. The tank was duly delivered back, and once refitted and pressure tested, XH558 could be fuelled up ready for our flight to Dunsfold.

All was progressing well as we climbed away from Doncaster, and Bill Perrins started to carry out a practice display prior to him doing the real thing at Dunsfold. During the display, the pilots noticed that the hydraulic pressure gauge was reading lower than it should be. I had a look through my periscope at the under surface of the aircraft to find that the starboard undercarriage door was not only drooping slightly, but was getting progressively worse. Martin abandoned the practice display and elected to fly back to Doncaster. We had just turned when the hydraulic pressure recovered and the starboard undercarriage door then closed flush as it should be. Thinking that all was now well, we turned back south again to continue on to Dunsfold, but only a few minutes after turning, Martin noticed that the hydraulic pressure was starting to fall yet again. Because it was continuing to fall we elected to lower the undercarriage whilst we still had enough hydraulic pressure to do so. Rather slowly and reluctantly, the undercarriage came down and after what seemed like an eternity, all the indications were that the wheels were safely down and locked. It was all starting to get just a bit anxious and so with Martin's permission, I declared an emergency on the radio and told Doncaster that we were diverting to RAF Coningsby in Lincolnshire.

As it was a weekend, RAF Coningsby was in a stand-by mode, although it can be fully active within a few minutes should the Typhoons based there get scrambled. Because they were not anticipating any scramble, the fire section were carrying out a training session on the airfield. In the middle of their training, they got a message from air traffic control to tell them that there was a Vulcan inbound, having declared an emergency with a hydraulic problem. Suddenly, their training session became the real thing.

As Martin successfully flew us onto the runway, Bill Perrins streamed the big brake parachute. I could see from looking through my periscope, that the fire engines were following us with their blue lights, flashing but more importantly, that the parachute had deployed successfully. All very dramatic. Because we had such low hydraulic pressure after using what little was left to lower the landing gear, Martin applied the brakes in one continuous braking action as per the book until we trundled to a halt. Unfortunately, by the time we stopped, we had run out of every last drop of hydraulic pressure. This presented a bit of a problem, because the hydraulics control the nose wheel steering and now we couldn't turn the nose wheel to vacate the runway. With no other option, we had to shut the aircraft down on the runway. Opening the door, I was met by Sgt Steve Parsons and his fire crew who set about making the aircraft safe. I could see a steady stream of hydraulic fluid pouring onto the runway from just aft of the nose wheel area, and Steve and his team immediately set about putting drip trays and absorbent paper towels down to catch the majority of the fluid.

Taff and his team worked their socks off at Coningsby to get the aircraft serviceable for the displays at Portrush in Northern Ireland and Cosby, Leicestershire on 4 September. After days and hours of blood, sweat and tears and much burning of the midnight oil, they resolved the hydraulic malfunction and declared the aircraft serviceable on the Friday, the day before 558 was due to do her 'overseas' trip. As the day dawned the weather wasn't looking too promising. There was a chance that we might just be able to do the displays before two major weather fronts coming in off the Atlantic were going to cover the UK as a whole, but no sooner had we had got up to the engine start section of the flight checks when the heavens opened. This was not looking good. We sat in the aircraft in the dry, while the ground crew tried to shelter under the wings and fuselage (sometimes known as the world's biggest umbrella), but the rain was so heavy it just entered all the nooks and crannies and emptied down on them no matter where they stood. The whole of Lincolnshire was in a deluge, so we had no option but to sit tight, until a break in the weather came which would allow us to do a mad dash across the Irish Sea and back. Martin also had to ensure that the weather at Doncaster would be ok for the time that we were due to land, and that wasn't looking too good either.

Time was rapidly running out on us, and eventually it became a physical impossibility for us to take off and get to Portrush in time to display before their show came to a close, even if the weather allowed us to. We had already run out of time to do the Cosby display and so, with a very heavy heart, Martin made the only decision

he could, and that was to call it a day and cancel the flight. We felt really terrible, we had a serviceable aircraft with sufficient fuel to perform the task; engineers who had performed miracles to get the aircraft ready for us; all we were lacking was decent weather in which to fly.

You could have heard the sigh of relief all across Lincolnshire, as XH558 lifted off from RAF Coningsby on 10 September for her flight up to RAF Leuchars in Scotland, and her last display of the season. After the traumatic and very disappointing previous few weeks, all our hopes were now pinned on the aircraft finishing the display season on a high. The crew comprised of Martin, Phill O'Dell and me, and, with the comforting howl of the four Olympus engines in our ears, we roared off down the runway and lifted off for our flight north.

Phill was going to do the display at Leuchars and, having not displayed the aircraft for some little while, he required a practice before he did the real thing. We set course for Elvington, the home of the Yorkshire Air Museum near York, where Martin had made arrangements for us to do the practice. It went well and we continued our journey north, and arrived at Leuchars on time ready for our display slot. Reports I've read indicate that the display was very well received and, once again, was one of the highlights of the display programme, eclipsed only by the appearance of the Red Arrows in an eight ship formation; their usual nine ship formation reduced by the tragic loss of one of their pilots at the Bournemouth show. Our display complete, we headed back home southwards to Doncaster to be met by our engineers, with smiles the width of Yorkshire. The season had come to an end on a high note, with a very successful display at Leuchars, and delivering a serviceable aircraft back into the hands of our hard working engineers was a bonus.

Over the Oxfordshire countryside.
Eric Coeckelberghs/aviation-photocrew.com

Above: Winter servicing in
the hangar at Doncaster.
Below: Taff Stone places the
'Salute to Her Majesty' book
in the cockpit.

XH558's flying season in 2012 was dedicated to the Diamond Jubilee of Her Majesty Queen Elizabeth II, and the 60th anniversary of the Avro Vulcan. As part of the *'Salute to Her Majesty'* a book of good wishes from supporters was carried on board, to be presented to The Queen at the end of the year.

Barry Masefield continues his blog as XH558 returns to the air for a special year.

2012

The waiting was over. At last, Taff Stone and his team of engineers had finished sufficient of the winter servicing schedule to enable XH558 to be taken for a test flight. All the hard work of his engineers, and the funding provided by our faithful public, was now going to be put to the test.

The crew to fly the air test was led by Kevin Rumens, who was also to be the aircraft Captain. He was to be accompanied by Paul Mulcahy, the CAA chief test pilot. Paul has done all the necessary test flights on XH558 over the past five years, and is always a welcome visitor to the project. Acting as AEO, and ensuring the electrical integrity of the aircraft down the back, was Phil Davies, while I sat in the Nav. Radar seat acting as the Flight Test Observer - which involved filling in all the results of the Flight Tests that we were going to be carrying out.

As could be expected, there was a large gathering of the media, not only to witness the air test but also to do interviews with us all about the 30th Anniversary of the Falklands War. As you will be aware, Martin and I flew the bombing missions, but Andy Marson was instrumental in planning the raids while working behind the scenes at RAF Waddington. Interviews concluded, we made our way to the aircraft, only to see the most awful black clouds developing and heading our way. The media were all lined up near the aircraft, ready to film us climbing aboard and then the heavens opened, resulting in a mad dash by the TV crews to scramble back on

Andrew Brown

the coach. We meanwhile, carried on and boarded the aircraft to get the show started. It was still chucking it down, but as soon as Phil called for clearance for us to move our resident guardian angel took over, and stopped the rain. We could see that there were sufficient breaks in the clouds to allow us to climb up through them, so we roared off down the runway, wheels were selected up, timings were noted for each individual wheel to indicate that it was safely stowed in the undercarriage bays, and up we climbed to 14,000 feet. I was making notes of various engine readings as we climbed, Phil Davies was chatting away on the radios, the two pilots were talking in their own language as pilots do, and soon we were levelling out at the top of the climb.

With the air test done it marked a major milestone reached. Taff Stone and his team of engineers had worked tirelessly over the winter months and XH558, declared fully serviceable by Paul, was testament to their professionalism and abilities. Of course, it wasn't just our engineers who had got us here. We must not lose sight of the fact that this is a team effort by everyone involved with the VTTST, and most of all, YOU, the great British public.

Falklands Memorial

It had been 30 years in the making but, finally, on Sunday May 20 SAMA 82 (South Atlantic Medal Association) unveiled the memorial wall at the National Memorial Arboretum, dedicated to the fallen from the Falklands War in 1982. We, the last remaining flying Vulcan, were graciously invited to help mark the event by completing a fly-over as the memorial was being unveiled. This was a poignant moment, not just for all the people who had been invited to attend the ceremony, but for the Vulcan crew too. Each and every one of us on the crew that day had participated either in the engineering, the planning or the flying of the Black Buck missions.

Overflying Trimpley Reservoir in the Severn Valley on the 2012 flypast tour. *Laurens van de Craats*

Very rarely do we fly with a navigator on board but on Sunday we needed to be over the Memorial on time, right to the second. We 'unwrapped' Andy Marson, our team navigator, dusted him off and got him airborne. Andy flew on the BBMF Lancaster and Dakota for seven years and was also a Tornado navigator, so is used to appearing over a target point accurate to the second. He was also a member of the mission planning team for Black Buck working in the Operation Wing at RAF Marham.

Our co-pilot on Sunday was Bill Perrins. Bill is a Virgin Atlantic Boeing 747 Captain, but he was also a Tornado F3 fighter pilot at the latter end of his RAF career. Back in 1982 he was also co-pilot to Alastair (Monty) Montgomery, who was captain of one of the crews to be selected for the Black Buck bombing missions.

Martin Withers was our captain on Sunday. There's not much more I can write about Martin which hasn't already been written. What I do know was that to achieve the permission to fly over the assembled guests at the Memorial required many hours of work, writing a Safety Case to allay any fears should something very unlikely go awry with the aircraft. Although he won't admit to it, I know that Sunday was a very special occasion for him as indeed, it was to the rest of our crew that day.

Finally, I come on to me. You all know what I did during the Falklands War so I shan't repeat it again. Just to say that it was a great honour back in 1982 to be selected to be with Squadron Leader John Reeve as the primary Vulcan crew on Black Buck One. Unfortunately, things didn't go our way that night, resulting in Martin Withers and his crew flying the mission in its entirety.

For each and every one of us in our own way it was a special day. We each had our own memories of that time back in 1982, as did everyone assembled on the ground at the Memorial. A lot of the guests on that day had tragically lost someone dear to them during that war. Fortunately, all of us associated with the Vulcan element of that War suffered no losses. I have met many Islanders since the war who were living on the Falklands at the time, and also numerous ex military personnel who served down in the South Atlantic, both on the ground and at sea in the Royal Navy. Every one of them has said to me that, without the Black Buck bombing and missile missions, The Falklands War may well have turned out very differently, and they remain forever grateful to the Vulcan force for their part in securing victory.

Don't Mess With The Gods

We're continually paying homage to Vulcan, the Roman god of fire and rightly so, perhaps then we can be forgiven for becoming just a little bit blinkered and forgetting about all the other gods that may, or may not, play a part in each of our lives. They are also looking down on us, and any slight transgression will result in them taking their revenge. And so they did, with a vengeance, on Friday 6 July when our crew comprising Martin Withers, Phill O'Dell and me attempted to get airborne and fly 558 to the Royal International Air Tattoo at Fairford, via Farnborough. We had been unforgivingly remiss, and none of us had given thanks to the most senior of the Greek gods - Zeus, the god of wind and rain.

As dawn broke, the heavens were unloading sheets of continuous rain. Now, we aircrew tend to be glass half full types of guys, so we assembled in the office at Robin Hood airfield to plan the day's trip, full of confidence that there was no way that the rain would continue to bucket down. However, our take off time came and went Zeus was still exacting his revenge. Talk about knitting with smoke – as soon as the weather at Farnborough became within our limits to display, the weather at Fairford would go out of limits, and vice versa. After waiting around all day, the weather cleared and we could have a go at flying southwards.

The aircraft was splendid and shiny with her new coat of paint, but looked as though she had been through a power wash, and water was dripping from the many orifices under the wings and fuselage. I was a bit concerned that water may have ingressed into the power compartment under the rudder area, where all of the electrical systems are controlled. This is a known area for water to accumulate if heavy rain has fallen, and there is the danger it will result in arcing and sparking amongst the electrical relays.

Below: New paintwork gleaming. Alex Golz

Opposite: Wingover at Fairford. Andrew Brown

Opposite bottom: Aircraft tours at Fairford. Andrew Brown

I was about to mention to Taff that I would like to ensure that his guys had mopped up in there, when he pre-empted me by assuring me they had just finished drying it all out, just as we were on our way to the aircraft. Why is he always one step ahead of me! Perhaps it's all those years of working together, and he now knows how my thinking goes.

The start checks were going well, until we got as far as the flying controls, when things started to go awry. For reasons best known to itself the rudder flying controls didn't want to play nicely. Between us, Taff and I checked the fuses, me in the cockpit checking the 28 volt ones and he in the power compartment checking the big 200 volt AC fuses. Eventually, we ran out of time for us to make our arrivals at both Farnborough and Fairford, so Martin had to make the painful decision for us all to climb out and try again in the morning. All very frustrating, Martin and Phill had spent all day on their mobiles arranging and re-arranging timings as the weather changed, and then we were thwarted by a technical problem, possibly due to the heavy rain.

The next morning Zeus was behaving himself, and once again we assembled at the now serviceable aircraft and very soon were taxiing out for a timed take off. One can only imagine the sighs of relief from Taff and the engineering team when they saw us get airborne. He could at last get all his engineering stuff together and drive off to meet us at Fairford.

At our briefing, we noticed that our route was to take us a few miles to the east of Silverstone. It was, of course, the weekend of the British Grand Prix and as we got closer to Silverstone I called the helicopter air traffic controller on the radio to let him know that we going to pass to the east but, with his permission, we were more than happy to do a fly-by over the race track. To say that the man was enthusiastic would be an understatement!

Continuing on south we eventually arrived at Farnborough. The purpose of going there was so Phill O'Dell could do a validation display in front of the Flying Control Committee. He flew a very impressive display and, as we were leaving to fly to Fairford, I got a message over the radio to say that his display had been approved. That set us up nicely for our next event in about 20 minutes time, which was to be a display at Fairford, to be flown once again by Phill. Those of you who were there all know that Phill gave a truly stunning display and, after we had landed, we were apparently met with rapturous applause. Of course, we can never hear that from inside the aircraft, but it's really gratifying when the crowd come up to us afterwards to tell us what they thought of the performance. Once the engines had been shut down and we could climb out of the cockpit, XH558 was towed to a position close to the Vulcan Village, where the crowd could have good photographic opportunities of her.

After a debrief with John Hufton, our crew chief for the arrival, it was but a short walk to the Vulcan Village to have a well earned cup of tea and mingle amongst the crowds in the tent, signing books and photos and just about anything else that they had been buying. The Vulcan Village was really busy for the whole of the weekend and the volunteers selling merchandise were working their socks off, helped for the weekend by Laura Withers and my partner, Rae. As the day progressed we were visited by many VIPs, including our very own Trustee, Mr Gerald Howarth, now Sir Gerald, MP. He brought along the Secretary of State for Defence, Philip Hammond MP. Martin and I took them both to the aircraft for a personal tour and, as always, those who have never been inside the aircraft before are amazed that we spent close on 16 hours in such a cramped environment during our Black Buck missions. We were visited by many of the other display teams, all of whom wanted photographs taken with them in front of the aircraft. It had turned out to be a great day, with the VTTST making lots of new friends and reacquainting with old relationships.

Sunday morning arrived and by 9am we were back at the Vulcan Village tent ready to fly. The pilots for the Sunday display were Kev Rumens and Bill Ramsey, plus me down the back in the 'coal hole'. Kev flew a really remarkable display, and between him and Bill they made the aircraft perform to its best. Down the back I watched with awe through my window and periscope as the horizon tilted left and right, up and down, and it was a truly exhilarating experience. People often ask me what it must be like down the back, they think I must be thrown around like a rag doll unless I'm well strapped in and are truly stunned when I tell them that, if the pilots fly the aircraft properly, there are very few uncomfortable moments during the display.

The next day was an early start for the crew of Kev, Bill, Phil Davies, and Andy Marson, the navigator for the day, who were to be up at 6am for the flight to Farnborough. They were to meet up with the Red Arrows en route and fly in formation to open the show, and after that to do some formation work with the Blades formation team and the lucky people who were passengers in their aircraft.

Opening the show at Farnborough with the Red Arrows. *Robert Pleming*

For me the weekend had drawn to a close. It had been a great weekend, interspersed with extreme highs and desperate lows. The highs were memorable, the lows were awful. So what did I learn from the weekend? For a start, if ever in the future the weather looks marginal I shall have a quiet word with Zeus, I must make sure that I never ever again mess with the gods!!

The Diamond Jubilee Flypast

Despite a previous attempt to fly a celebration flypast for the Queen's Diamond Jubilee, events had conspired against us. We had intended to overfly the Royal Barge during the River Thames pageant, but having lost a couple of engines in an incident a few days before the official Diamond Jubilee day, XH558 was grounded while our techies replaced the engines. As it so happened the weather would have prevented us flying over the pageant anyway, with steady continuous rain and very low cloud shrouding the event.

However, on 18 July, we succeeded. The VTTST had been in contact with the Royal Household, and they had approved a flypast by the Vulcan while Her Majesty was visiting the North East of England as part of her Diamond Jubilee Tour of the United Kingdom. The Queen and Prince Phillip were to spend the night on a luxury boat, the Leander, in Sunderland docks before undertaking their royal duties the following day around the North East. Just before they were due to step ashore at 10am we were to overfly them at 1,000 feet. We roared overhead, and Martin carried out a full power spiral climb to let all of Sunderland people know we had arrived. We completed one orbit around the Royal party and then departed southwards. Job done.

We then headed to Elvington, where Martin was going to carry out practice displays. It was at this juncture in this 'Royal' sortie that I felt the call of nature, and decided to carry out the necessary, just as Martin started his first wing-over. He was performing a tricky manoeuvre but not half as tricky as the manoeuvre I was trying to perform, it lent a whole new meaning to the 'Royal Wee'! Kev meanwhile, was beside himself with laughter, as he looked down at his AEO struggling valiantly to maintain not only his balance but a sense of decorum. One would think that, after all these years of display flying, I would know better than to try that sort of thing during a display practice.

Holidays at the seaside

August was almost like being on holiday. We were scheduled to appear at Eastbourne, the Clacton seaside show (a new venue for us) and at several venues in the south of England, including the Wings & Wheels air show at Dunsfold, and a visit to a show near Basingstoke which was being held in aid of Children In Need. Finally, we were to appear at another small event at Little Gransden near Huntingdon.

Being down in the Clacton area, and very close to Southend, it also gave us the opportunity to visit Vulcan XL426 which is parked at Southend airport. The supporters of 426 have always been supportive of 558 and it felt only right that this very day, being the 50th birthday of 426, we should visit her to say 'happy birthday'.

The following weekend was to see us flying back south to appear at the Dunsfold Wings & Wheels air show. We always look forward to this event because, not only do we get to appear at the home of the Top Gear show, we also get the opportunity to fly over Eddie Forrester's house, which is very close to Dunsfold airfield. Eddie has been our guardian angel right from the start of 558 flying on the air show circuit. When things were dire, and we were looking over the edge of the financial abyss, Eddie has on many occasions stepped in with generous donations to keep us going.

Looking out my side window at the airfield, I could see that there was a considerable crowd gathered. It never ceases to amaze me to see the thousands of faces looking skyward as we fly in to commence our display. The pilots that day were Kev Rumens and Martin Withers, and between them they put on yet another stunning display. Although the display routine remains the same throughout every display, there are some displays when I get the feeling from inside the cockpit that this display is a real stunner, and Saturday's was one of those occasions. I'm sure that the crowd must have been ecstatic; I know I was, and I've been doing this for nearly 25 years.

We left Dunsfold and headed off to our next venue near Basingstoke. This was the Chris Evans CarFest show, which was being held in aid of the BBC's Children In Need appeal. After that we headed eastwards over to the Bedford/Huntingdon area, to do a few passes at another charity event at Little Gransden. This done, it was time to head north for our return to Doncaster. It had been yet another good day. Not only did we perform stunningly at Dunsfold but we had an opportunity to say thank you to Eddie, and lastly help to support the Children In Need appeal. What better use of your aircraft eh!

Vulcan and Pudsey at Little Gransden. *David Poile*

Main photo: Flying over Clacton's wind turbines. *Andrew Brown*

It was time to put the bucket and spade away until my next visit to the seaside, our displays at both Bournemouth and Shoreham the next weekend. After a great day on Saturday at the Bournemouth seaside air show, when XH558, flown by Martin Withers, Bill Ramsey and Phil Davies, followed up their first display with a further air show at Shoreham - it was somewhat of a disappointment that on the Sunday, the weather took a turn for the worse.

The plan for the day was for us to transit down to the south coast, fly a display at Bournemouth, then transit along the coast to Shoreham, where we were to meet up with the Blades display team before flying in formation over the Shoreham display venue. We would then transit up to Dunsfold airfield, where Bill Ramsey was going to fly a practice display, with a display examiner from the CAA observing from the ground. If Bill's display was deemed to be satisfactory, then he would be given authority to carry out Vulcan displays for the next 12 months. That was the plan!

As we flew along the beach at Bournemouth, I could see that even though the weather wasn't fine and sunny like the day previous, a massive crowd had assembled. All too soon, the display was over and we cleared from the Bournemouth display area to head east towards Worthing pier, where we were going to meet up with the Blades. We hugged the coast all the way up and finally the pilots could see the pier a few miles ahead. The weather was starting to get a little murky by this time but still within our limits. The Blades hove into view, a few hundred yards astern and to the port side. Martin cleared them to join us in formation and we continued on until, as we overflew Shoreham airfield, the Blades switched on their smoke to complete the spectacle. The Blades broke formation and now, on our own, Martin started his display - but it soon became evident that the weather was closing in quite rapidly. Just to the north of the airfield is a range of hills which we needed to have in sight continuously, but they were becoming obscured in the cloud and, after attempting a few orbits around the display venue, Martin very wisely decided that the weather was outside our limits and called a halt to proceedings.

We decided that the best bet was to return to Doncaster and try and get Bill's authorisation another day. However, life isn't that easy. Our planned return route was by this time denied to us because of the weather, so we had to come up with an alternative plan. It soon became apparent that the best route would be to continue along the south coast towards Kent, before turning north towards Clacton, Mildenhall, Wisbech, and Waddington, then finally into Doncaster. Bill checked out the fuel situation to see whether we would have sufficient to fly the route, I meanwhile plotted the various turning points we needed to fly over, and Martin flew the aircraft to keep us safely clear of the coast. It has always been said that 'flexibility is the cornerstone of air power', and this was flexibility in action.

Below: Rounding Beach Head for the Eastbourne show. *Andrew Brown*

Opposite top: Over the sea at Eastbourne. *Andrew Brown*

Opposite bottom: In the company of The Blades and Spitfire, Sywell. *Charles Toop*

It had been an eventful day. Because we had anticipated that the weather might turn against us, and force a re-route upon us, it didn't come as too much of a shock when the situation became a reality. Just goes to show, that flexibility and planning provides the solution to most situations that life may throw at us.

The season draws to a close

Vulcan XH558 completed her last commercial display for the 2012 season with a display at RAF Leuchars, but she hadn't quite finished her flying for the year. On 20th September, a crew comprising Kev Rumens, Bill Ramsey, myself and Martin Andrews (Junior), flew a private trip to Sywell (Northampton) aerodrome where we were to do some formation flying with the Blades team and a Spitfire. Our long-term friend and erstwhile saviour, Eddie Forrester, had organised and paid for the Blades to fly some passengers alongside 558. The lucky winners of the raffle that the Trust had organised over the summer months were also there, to experience the delight of flying with the Blades alongside us - but, the star prize had to be the winner who won a seat in a Spitfire to fly alongside us too.

A couple of years ago, the children at Great Doddington primary school completed a project to help with the funding of 558, and while I was at breakfast I received a text on my mobile phone from one of the teachers, Ellie, welcoming us back to the Sywell area and wishing us a safe flight. Well I can take a hint as well as the next man! I mentioned it to Kev and he could see no reason why we couldn't spare a few minutes to fly over the school. I let them know that we would be with them at 2-30pm and, to my surprise, was told that the school would effectively be shut down while all the children assembled in the playground to wave to us. Please don't tell Michael Gove, although I'm sure that he could be persuaded that this was all in aid of our aim of 'Inspiring a generation'.

Toni Hunter, our resident tour guide, organiser, chauffeur, administrator and any other job that may fall her way, then asked whether we could overfly Hayfield primary school on our way out of Doncaster.

Hayfield School is resident at Doncaster, right alongside the hangars, and was launching the new uniform, the school badge featuring the Vulcan as its centrepiece. Kev rang Doncaster air traffic control, to see if they would agree to us flying a non-standard departure in order to overfly the school and, like the man from Del Monte, they said 'yes' Once airborne, we flew back over the airfield before turning back in to fly over the school and the children, who were all waving from the playground. We could almost hear the squeals of delight from all those upturned faces.

Pressing on, we were soon at Sywell and could hear the Blades on the frequency, taxiing out to the runway. Soon, I could see them behind me in my periscope and, having told Kev and Bill that they were behind us, Kev cleared them to join us on either side. I could hear the noise of their engines running at full throttle as they flew alongside us, sounding like a swarm of angry bees. All too soon the formation work came to an end, and we continued on down to Great Doddington primary school to see our young admirers. Kev identified the school and flew over not once, but three times. On our final pass he waggled the wings and that gave me the opportunity, when the port wing was down, to see all the kiddies waving furiously at us. I don't know what it is, but it always gives me a warm glow inside when I see these youngsters showing such great enthusiasm with their waving arms. I guess that it takes me back to when I was the same age - when I used to wave at aircraft whenever they passed low over me. It was that thrill I got, when waving to the aircraft all those years ago as they passed low overhead, that imbued in me a love of aircraft, and set me on the path to a career in aviation.

Icons of England.
2Excel Aviation

With the school visit complete, we ventured on down south a further 20 miles to Cranfield, where Bill completed his practice display, whereupon we set course back to the Pitsford lakes to meet up with the Blades for our second episode of formation flying. Once again the 'angry bees' closed on us, and I could also see the Spitfire momentarily below us through my periscope before he went out of my field of vision. The formation work was soon finished and Kev then flew a display over the airfield, before we bid Sywell and the spectators goodbye and set off northbound to Doncaster. For me, the best part of the day was the fact that we were able to let the school children experience the very awesome presence of the Vulcan, and hope that, just maybe, it will fill them with enthusiasm which will manifest itself by them coming into the world of aviation in their adult lives. If that happens, then our motto of "inspire a generation" will have been achieved.

A Triumphant Day

Saturday 29 September was the day of XH558's final flight for 2012. It was a day that, for those of us who fly the aircraft, was tinged with a certain amount of sadness. I've said many times before that we aircrew are never happier than when we have 558 strutting her stuff up where she belongs, and to know that she is going to be taken away from us for the next six months or so is quite saddening.

The trip was designed to celebrate the 60th anniversary of the first flight of the Vulcan and, to make the sortie special, we were to visit many factories, airfields and institutions that have been associated with the Vulcan over those six decades. The crew comprised of Bill Ramsey, who was captain for the day, Kev Rumens as co-pilot, Andy Marson our navigator, and yours truly as the AEO. We headed south to overfly the Newark Aviation Museum, the venue for the bi-annual V Force reunion, before continuing on to Bitteswell, which in years past had been the main Vulcan maintenance unit. From there we flew over Coventry Airport, where the Vulcan Crew Chiefs Register were holding their annual reunion, before turning north west to then overfly Birmingham

Airport, and on to RAF Cosford. Having flown over those airfields, our route was to then take us southwards, towards Gloucester Staverton Airfield. It was on this leg that we had planned to do some air-to-air photography with some aviation photographers aboard a Skyvan aircraft. Because of the incompatibilities of our respective airspeeds it can be quite tricky, the Skyvan is going at full speed while we're virtually falling out of the sky because we're going so slowly! Slight exaggeration but you get the gist of what I mean.

After Gloucester, we had to be at Kemble at a specified time for Bill Ramsey to perform a display in front of an authorised CAA examiner, in order to obtain his display qualification for the 2013 display season. We continued our flight profile, which then took us out over the Bristol Channel before turning south to overfly Bristol Filton. Filton, of course, has a long affinity with the Vulcan, it being the home of the Rolls-Royce establishment in days past where our Olympus engines were tried and tested. Not only that, some of you will recall that it was out of Filton that the Vulcan flew with the test version of the Concorde Rolls-Royce Olympus engine strapped underneath. That fly though completed, Bristol Lulsgate was our next destination for a fly by.

It was now time to go 'overseas', and head back out across the Bristol Channel to Cardiff airport, before we then flew a few more miles to what was RAF St. Athan, for many years the home of the big maintenance unit tasked with the deep servicing of the RAF's V force aircraft. Heading north from St Athan, we passed up through Wales towards the Brecon Beacons. The weather was glorious and we could see for miles. I stood on the ladder between the pilots to witness the view of the hills that I had walked over on many occasions. We could see walkers on the top of Pen-Y-Fan, who would have had a magnificent sight of us as we flew past beneath them.

Above: Flypast at Staverton, Gloucestershire. *Ian Waudby*

Below: Over the countryside near Ross-on-Wye. *Stuart Wilding*

The Beacons slipped behind us as we continued flying northbound, passing Hereford before turning south to head towards the main event of the day – a fly-by of a memorial service held in memory of a friend and client of Eddie Forrester, our long term supporter and benefactor. This was being held in the small settlement of Bishopswood near Ross-on-Wye, nestled alongside the river in the base of a steep-sided valley. We had seen satellite imagery of the venue, and were fully aware that there was high ground all around us. It looked from the photos that the Memorial Hall was going to be difficult to spot but, as we flew down the valley, it soon became readily apparent, because the pilots could see lots of camera flash guns flashing as we approached the venue. We completed a run past, before climbing up above the top of the valley to go around again and repeat the process. The second run was completed with a full power climb away and, from what I hear, the noise, being contained within the confines of the valley sides, was absolutely deafening. I'm sure that all who were there couldn't have failed to be impressed.

Onwards we flew, towards Brize Norton for the over flight there to say a big 'thank you' for the help they all gave us during our first couple of seasons, when we were searching for a permanent home for 558. Without the help and enthusiasm from their Station Commander, and the rest of his Station personnel, it is debatable whether the VTTST would have been able to continue. As Brize receded into

Charles Toop

the distance behind us, we had just one more venue to visit in the south of the country before commencing our journey northwards and home.

RAF Halton has been the home of aircraft engineering since time immemorial, and it has seen thousands of Vulcan aircraft technicians pass through its portals, before going on to do their valuable work during the tense years of the Cold War. Without that centre of engineering excellence, producing engineers of the highest calibre, the country would have been poorly placed over those dark years. It was only right that 558 should pay her respects to RAF Halton and all who have served there, either as instructors or students of engineering.

On our way back home it would have been churlish not to have visited both RAF Scampton and Waddington which were, for so many years, the homes to many Vulcan squadrons before they were disbanded. As our tour came to its conclusion, we thought that it would be a fitting tribute to all of the staff at Robin Hood in all departments, and to all those supporters who were lining the airfield perimeter, if we were to do a fly by for them too. The air traffic controller cleared us in for a run and break, after which full power was applied for a steep turn, before heading back towards the runway for our final landing of 2012. Wheels were selected down and, finally, 558 settled on the runway after a 3¼ hour trip, ready for a well earned rest over the winter months.

It had been a great season for XH558. Once our initial engineering difficulties had been resolved, she flew every display that was asked of her, and remained fully serviceable throughout. This is an incredible achievement for an aircraft of her vintage. Finally, without you our faithful fans, none of this would have been possible. Your donations have kept 558 up where she belongs, and you should all be very proud of yourselves and your achievement. On a personal note, I would like to say thank you to you all for donating your hard earned cash, which allows me and my aircrew colleagues the privilege of flying your aircraft.

See you in 2013.
Barry Masefield

Opposite: Over the West Midlands.
Laurens van de Craats

Below: Air-to-air on the Flypast tour.
Frank Grealish/irishairpics.com

Avro Type 707

Avro Type 707 **VX784**

In November 1948 Specification E.15/48 was issued calling for a 1/3 scale model of the type 698 to investigate low-speed stability and control characteristics. VX784 was completed in August 1949, fitted with a Rolls-Royce Derwent 5 engine giving a 3,500lbs thrust. Construction utilised the undercarriage from an Avro Athena trainer, and the nosewheel and cockpit canopy from the Meteor. Taxiing trials were held at Woodford before a transfer to A&AEE. First flight of the first British delta wing aircraft was on 4 September 1949 at Boscombe Down. The pilot was Flight Lieutenant S. Eric Esler DFC. During a subsequent low-speed low-flying trial test flight from Farnborough the aircraft crashed; Esler was killed.

Avro Type 707B **VX790**

Completed in August 1950 and fitted with a Rolls-Royce Derwent 5 engine producing 3,500lbs thrust. Following the crash of VX784 a Martin Baker ejector seat was installed as well as a new cockpit canopy, the nosewheel from a Hawker Sea Hawk and the airbrake system moved to the upper wing surface. Chief Test Pilot Wing Commander Roland J 'Roly' Falk OBE DFC made its first flight on 6 September 1950. In January 1956 the aircraft was transferred to the Empire Test Pilot School for test-pilot training. It later suffered an accident when landing at RAE Farnborough. The pilot, Flight Lieutenant B.A. Ashley was unhurt but the aircraft sustained Cat. (5) damage and was stored at No.71 MU, Bicester before being struck off charge in November 1957 and used for spares.

Avro Type 707A **WD280**

The first of two 707As, WD280 was designed to fly at high subsonic Mach numbers and had a scaled-down Type 698 wing and air intakes situated at the wing roots (both previous 707s had a dorsal intake). Powered by a Rolls-Royce Derwent 8 engine producing 3,600lbs thrust the aircraft first flew from Boscombe Down on 14 June 1951 piloted by 'Roly' Falk. To overcome stability problems the manual controls were replaced with a powered system. WD280 was used intensively to investigate buffeting that began to threaten the larger Type 698 programme, and in 1954 was fitted with a modified wing with a kinked leading edge. After successful testing this later became the Vulcan 'Phase Two' wing modification. WD280 was acquired by the Royal Australian Airforce Aircraft Research and Development Unit and shipped to Sydney in HMAS Melbourne arriving on 1 May 1956. Transferred to RAAF Laverton it was used in a variety of tests, finally retiring during 1963. WD280 was auctioned into private hands in 1967 but returned to RAAF Museum, Point Cooke, Victoria in 1999.

Avro Type 707A WZ736

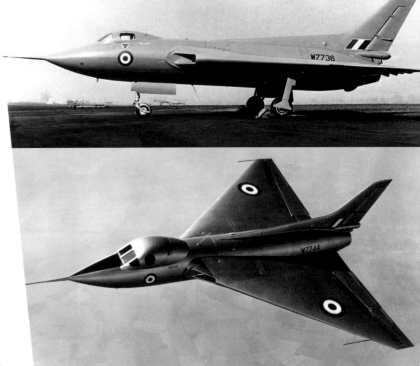

The second 707A to specification E.10/49 was built at Avro's repair site at Bracebridge Heath, Lincolnshire and first flew from RAF Waddington piloted by American Sqn Ldr J C Nelson on 20th February 1953. The aircraft was flown to Woodford and remained there for production acceptance testing before being handed over to the Royal Aircraft Establishment (RAE). Powered flying controls were installed at Woodford in April 1954 with trials carried out at RAE Farnborough and the Armament and Instrument Experimental Unit (AIEU), Martlesham Heath. WZ736 was then involved in auto-throttle development trials at RAE Bedford until withdrawn in 1964. The aircraft survives in the Museum of Science and Industry at Manchester.

Avro Type 707C WZ744

The last 707 to be built, WZ744 first flew from RAF Waddington on 1 July 1953 piloted by Avro test pilot Squadron Leader Jack Wales. Like WZ736 this aircraft was also built at Bracebridge Heath, its dual control side-by-side controls squeezed into the small cockpit left no room for ejector seats. A new all metal canopy was fitted incorporating circular side windows. All four 707s and the two prototype Vulcans VX770 and VX777 flew in formation at the 1953 Farnborough airshow. The 707Cs were intend to familiarise pilots with the characteristics of delta-winged aircraft, but the early Vulcans proved easy to fly and a second planned aircraft WZ739 was later cancelled. WZ744 flew nearly 200 hours in the development of fly-by-wire electrically signalled hydraulic flying controls until June 1966. After a period of storage it was transferred to RAF Colerne for museum display, finally ending up at the RAF Museum at Cosford.

Avro Type 698 Prototypes

Prototype Vulcan VX770

Contract 6/Air/1942/CB.6(a). Dated 6 July 1948. First flight 30 August 1952. Delivered in August 1952 and fitted initially with Rolls-Royce Avon engines, later with Sapphires and finally Conways. Used by A&AEE Boscombe Down and manufacturer for trials. Suffered a mid-air explosion due to structural failure at Syerston on 20 September 1958 and was destroyed.

Prototype Vulcan VX777

Contract 6/Air/1942/CB.6(a). Dated 6 July 1948. First flight 3 September 1953. Delivered in September 1953, fitted with Olympus 100 engines. Trials aircraft for high altitude, radio and radar testing. Suffered Cat 3 damage on an overshoot landing on 27 July 1954. Resumed test flying on 23 March 1955, fitted with Olympus 101 engines. Converted to prototype B Mk.2, making a first flight in this configuration on 31 August 1957. Last flight on 27 April 1960, then used for non-flying runway trials with the RAE. Broken up at Farnborough in July 1963.

Photos in the sections on aircraft serials are assumed to be Avro or MoD/Crown Copyright unless stated otherwise.

Avro Vulcan XA serials

Vulcan B Mk.1 XA889

The first production B Mk.1, delivered on 4 February 1955 fitted with Olympus 101 engines, later replaced with 102 and 104s. Returned to Avro in 1956 for Mod.84 (kinked and drooped leading edge to wings) and fitted with vortex generators in front of the ailerons and auto-stabilisation system. Used on A&AEE Trials and Bristol Siddeley trials at Patchway. Withdrawn in 1967 and scrapped at Boscombe Down in 1971.

Vulcan B Mk.1 XA890

Delivered in 1955 and fitted with Olympus 104 engines. Displayed at Farnborough SBAC show in 1955, pilot Roly Falk performed an upward barrel roll. Returned to Avro in 1956 for Mod.84 (kinked and drooped leading edge to wings). Used at A&AEE, RAE Farnborough /Bedford and Thurleigh for manufacturers trials, radio and radar trials, blind landing trials and ballistics research, including conventional and nuclear weapons. Withdrawn and scrapped at Bedford in 1971.

Vulcan B Mk.1 XA891

Delivered in September 1955 and fitted with Olympus 104 engines. Used on A&AEE trials and Bristol Siddeley trials at Patchway with Olympus 200 series engines. RAE trials at Farnborough and Manufacturers trials. Crashed on a test flight near Hull on 24 July 1959 due to an electrical failure, crew all abandoned the aircraft successfully.

BAE Systems

Vulcan B Mk.1 **XA892**

Delivered in 1955 and fitted with Olympus 104 engines. Manufacturers trials and A&AEE armament trials. Modified in 1960 at Woodford for carriage and dropping of nuclear weapons. Delivered to RAF Halton in 1961 for ground instruction as No.(7746M) and scrapped in 1972.

Vulcan B Mk.1 **XA893**

Delivered in January 1956 and fitted with Olympus 104 engines. Used for A&AEE electrical trials connected with B Mk.2 variant (including ram air turbine and Rover AAPP - the only B Mk.1 to be fitted with them) and radio countermeasures (RCM) trials. Fitted with prototype fairings for carriage of Blue Steel missile at Hucclecote works of Gloster Aircraft. Broken up at Boscombe Down in 1962. Nose section transferred to 71 Maintenance Unit at Bicester.

Vulcan B Mk.1 **XA894**

Delivered in January 1957 and fitted with Olympus 104 engines. A&AEE trials (Mk.10 autopilot and anti-icing), engine development trials. From 1960, operated by Bristol Siddeley at Patchway as engine test bed for Olympus 22R as part of TSR2 trials programme. Destroyed in a fire while ground running at Patchway on 3 December 1962 after LP turbine disc failed.

Rolls-Royce

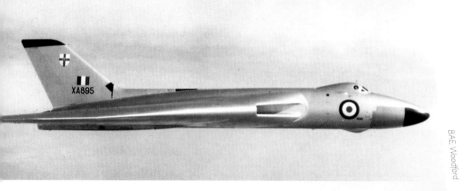

BAE Woodford

Vulcan B Mk.1 **XA895**

Delivered on 16 August 1956 and fitted with Olympus 104 engines. Converted to B Mk.1A in 1958. **Served with:** 230 Operational Conversion Unit (first Vulcan delivered into RAF service), Bomber Command Development Unit and A&AEE ECM trials. Withdrawn on 13 January 1967 and sold as scrap to Bradbury Ltd. on 19 September 1968.

Fred Martin

Vulcan B Mk.1 **XA896**

Delivered on 7 March 1957 and fitted with Olympus 104 engines. **Served with:** 230 OCU, 83 Squadron and 44 Squadron. Used as Bristol Siddeley test bed for BS100 vectored-thrust engine, intended for Hawker P.1154 supersonic fighter. Partially converted for this role until fighter development was abandoned. Withdrawn during 1966 and scrapped at Patchway.

Vulcan B Mk.1 **XA897**

Delivered on 20 July 56 and fitted with Olympus 104 Engines. **Served with:** 230 OCU and A&AEE trials. Embarked on a round-the-world goodwill tour to Australia and New Zealand to demonstration the range and capabilities of the aircraft, but crashed on its return during approach to Heathrow Airport on 1 October 1956 and was destroyed.

Vulcan B Mk.1 **XA898**

Delivered on 3 January 1957 and fitted with Olympus 104 engines. **Served with:** 230 OCU. Used exclusively by the OCU before being delivered to Halton on 25 August 1964 for use as an instructional airframe No.(7856M). Scrapped in 1971.

Vulcan B Mk.1 XA899

Delivered on 28 February 1957 and fitted with Olympus 104 engines. Used on A&AEE trials, RAE trials at Thurleigh, blind landing experiments at RAE Bedford and auto pilot development. First four-engined aircraft to make a fully automatic landing, on 22 December 1959. Delivered to RAF Cosford as instructional airframe No.(7812M). Scrapped in 1973. Nose section retained by Cosford Museum.

Vulcan B Mk.1 XA900

Delivered on 25 March 1957 and fitted with Olympus 104 engines. **Served with:** 230 OCU and 101 Squadron. Delivered to RAF Cosford as instructional airframe No.(7896M) in February 1966. Withdrawn from use and transferred to Cosford Museum as the last Vulcan B Mk.1. Scrapped during 1986 due to corrosion.

Vulcan B Mk.1 XA901

Delivered on 4 April 1957 and fitted with Olympus 104 engines. **Served with:** 230 OCU, 44 Squadron and 83 Squadron. Delivered to Cranwell as instructional airframe No.(7897M) in 1965. Scrapped in 1972.

Vulcan B Mk.1 XA902

Delivered on 10 May 1957 and fitted with Olympus/Conway/Spey engines. **Served with:** 230 OCU. Damaged in landing accident on 28 February 1958. Engine trials (Conway and Spey) with Rolls-Royce. Scrapped in 1963.

XA

Vulcan B Mk.1 **XA903**

Delivered on 31 May 1957 and fitted with Olympus 101 engines. Used for A&AEE and RAE Farnborough Blue Steel trials Aircraft. Delivered to Rolls-Royce as a test bed for Concorde Olympus and Tornado RB 199 engines. Experimental 27mm cannon fit at A&AEE. Made the last flight by a B.1 Vulcan at Farnborough on 22 February 1979. Scrapped in 1980.

Rolls-Royce

Vulcan B Mk.1 **XA904**

Delivered on 16 July 1957 and fitted with Olympus 104 engines. Converted to B.1A standard in 1960. **Served with:** 83 Squadron and 44 Squadron. Damaged in crash landing at Waddington on 1 March 1961 when three engines cut on second approach, due to low fuel after a 6½ hour sortie. Disposed as instructional airframe No.(7738M) and later scrapped.

Robin A Walker

Vulcan B Mk.1 **XA905**

Delivered on 11 July 1957 and fitted with Olympus 104 engines. Converted to B.1A standard in 1960. **Served with:** 83 Squadron (first Vulcan taken on charge by the squadron), 44 Squadron, 230 OCU and Waddington Wing (44/50/101 Squadrons). Delivered to Newton as an instructional airframe No.(7857M). Scrapped in 1974.

Vulcan B Mk.1 **XA906**

Delivered on 12 August 1957 and fitted with Olympus 104 engines. Converted to B.1A standard in 1962 at AWA Bitteswell. **Served with:** 83 Squadron, 44 Squadron and Waddington Wing. Stored at St. Athan from 10 March 1967 and sold as scrap to Bradley & Co. on 6 November 1968.

Robin A Walker

XA

Vulcan B Mk.1 **XA907**

Delivered on 29 August 1957 and fitted with Olympus 104 engines. Converted to B.1A. standard in 1961. **Served with:** 83 Squadron, 44 Squadron, Waddington Wing and BCDU Finningley. Withdrawn from use on 3 November 1966 and sold as scrap on 20 May 1968.

Vulcan B Mk.1 **XA908**

Delivered on 18 September 1957 and fitted with Olympus 104 engines. **Served with:** 83 Squadron. Toured Central Africa with XA904 and XA911 in 1958 after total electrical failure. Crashed in Michigan, USA on 24 October 1958.

Vulcan B Mk.1 **XA909**

Delivered on 1 October 1957 and fitted with Olympus 104 engines. Converted to B.1A standard in 1962. **Served with:** 101 Squadron, 50 Squadron Waddington Wing. Crashed on Anglesey on 16 July 1964 following an engine explosion, all crew escaped.

Vulcan B Mk.1 **XA910**

Delivered on 31 October 1957 and fitted with Olympus 104 engines. Converted to B.1A standard in 1962. **Served with:** 101 Squadron, 230 OCU, 50 Squadron and 44 Squadron. Became instructional airframe No. (7995M) at Cottesmore and later scrapped.

Fred Martin

Hugh Burt

Peter Middlebrook

Peter Middlebrook

Peter Middlebrook

Vulcan B Mk.1 **XA911**

Delivered on 1 November 1957 and fitted with Olympus 104 engines. Converted to B.1A standard in 1962. **Served with:** 83 Squadron, 230 OCU and Waddington Wing. Appeared as the star of the 1960 film 'Delta 8-3' about the V-Force. Delivered to St. Athan on 2 February 1967 and sold as scrap on 8 November 1968.

Vulcan B Mk.1 **XA912**

Delivered on 2 December 1957 and fitted with Olympus 104 engines. Converted to B.1A standard in 1960. **Served with:** 101 Squadron, Waddington Wing. Transferred to 19 MU St. Athan in March 1967. Sold as scrap on 20 May 1968.

Vulcan B Mk.1 **XA913**

Delivered on 19 December 1959 and fitted with Olympus 104 engines. Converted to B.1A standard in 1961. **Served with:** 101 Squadron, Waddington Wing. Appeared in the film Thunderball (1965). Stored at St. Athan on 21 December 1966 and sold as scrap on 20 May 1968.

Carmel J Attard

Avro Vulcan XH serials

Vulcan B Mk.1 **XH475**

Delivered in January 1958 and fitted with Olympus 104 engines. **Served with:** 230 OCU January 1958, 101 Squadron, Waddington Wing February 1958. Converted to B.1A standard in 1962. Finally became an instructional airframe No.(7996M) and scrapped in June 1969.

Vulcan B Mk.1 **XH476**

Delivered in February 1958 and fitted with Olympus 104 engines. Converted to B.1A standard in 1962. **Served with:** 101 Squadron and 44 Squadron. Withdrawn from service in May 1967 and sold as scrap on 21 January 1969.

XH

Vulcan B Mk.1 **XH477**

Delivered in February 1958 and fitted with Olympus 104 engines. Converted to B.1A standard in 1961. **Served with:** 83 Squadron, 44 Squadron and 50 Squadron. Crashed at St. Colme, Aboyne, Scotland. Flew into a hill during a low flying exercise, crew all killed. Struck off charge on 18 June 1963.

Vulcan B Mk.1 **XH478**

Delivered in March 1958 and fitted with Olympus 104 engines. Converted to B.1A standard in 1962. Used in Ministry of Aviation in-flight refuelling trials, testing the nose-mounted refuelling probe. **Served with:** Waddington Wing. Delivered to Akrotiri, Cyprus as instructional airframe (MC8047M) in March 1969. Later scrapped.

Vulcan B Mk.1 **XH479**

Delivered in March 1958 and fitted with Olympus 104 engines. Converted to B.1A standard in 1961. **Served with:** 101 Squadron and Waddington Wing. Delivered to Halton as instructional airframe No.(7974M) and scrapped in 1973.

Vulcan B Mk.1 **XH480**

Delivered in April 1958 and fitted with Olympus 104 engines. Converted to B.1A standard in 1962. **Served with:** 83 Squadron, 44 Squadron and Waddington Wing. Delivered to St. Athan in November 1966 and sold as scrap on 30 September 1968.

Vulcan B Mk.1 **XH481**

Delivered in April 1958 and fitted with Olympus 104 engines. Converted to B.1A standard in 1960. **Served with:** 101 Squadron and Waddington Wing. Made the first non-stop UK to Australia flight on 20-21 June 1961, covering 11,500 miles in 20 hours 3 minutes (an average speed of 573mph). Delivered to Cottesmore fire dump on 11 January 1968 and scrapped in 1977.

Vulcan B Mk.1 **XH482**

Delivered in May 1958 and fitted with Olympus 104 engines. Converted to B.1A standard in 1960. **Served with:** 617 Squadron, 50 Squadron, 101 Squadron and Waddington Wing. Delivered to St. Athan on 13 October 1966 and scrapped on 19 September 1968

Vulcan B Mk.1 **XH483**

Delivered in May 1958 and fitted with Olympus 104 engines. Converted to B.1A standard in 1961. **Served with:** 617 Squadron, 50 Squadron and Waddington Wing. Transferred to Manston fire dump on 3 August 1967 and scrapped in 1977.

Vulcan B Mk.1 **XH497**

Delivered in May 1958 and fitted with Olympus 104 engines. Converted to B.1A standard in 1962. **Served with:** 617 Squadron, 50 Squadron and Waddington Wing. Landing accident at Scampton on 3 July 1958 after nosewheel detached during take-off. Rear crew baled out before the pilot attempted the landing, sadly navigator was killed due to parachute failure. Moved to 19 MU in April 1966 and sold as scrap in January 1969.

Peter Middlebrook

XH

Vulcan B Mk.1 XH498

Delivered in June 1958 and fitted with Olympus 104 engines. Converted to B.1A standard in October 1961. **Served with:** 617 Squadron, 50 Squadron and Waddington Wing. Aircraft landed short at Rongotai, New Zealand on 25 October 1959 and broke the port landing gear, pilot able to get airborne and landed at RNZAF base at Ohakea with minimal damage to the airframe. Repaired by 3 January 1960 .Transferred to Finningley in 1967 as instructional airframe No.(7993M) and later scrapped.

Tony Milton

Vulcan B Mk.1 XH499

Delivered on 17 July 1958 and fitted with Olympus 104 engines. Converted to B.1A standard in 1962. **Served with:** 617 Squadron, 50 Squadron and 44 Squadron. Also used at HSAL Woodford and A&AEE. for low-level role equipment testing. Withdrawn from service in November 1965 and later scrapped at Bitteswell.

Vulcan B Mk.1 XH500

Delivered in August 1958 and fitted with Olympus 104 engines. Prototype conversion at AWA Bitteswell with XH505 to B.1A standard in July 1959, first Vulcan to be converted. **Served with:** 617 Squadron, BCDU, 50 Squadron and Waddington Wing. Allotted to RAF Scampton as instructional airframe No.(7994M). Scrapped in 1977.

Malcolm McCrow

Vulcan B Mk.1 XH501

Delivered in September 1958 and fitted with Olympus 104 engines. Converted to B.1A standard in March 1961. **Served with:** 617 Squadron, 44 Squadron, 50 Squadron and Waddington Wing. Delivered to St. Athan in March 1966 and sold as scrap to Bradbury & Co. in November 1968.

Geoffrey Smith

XH

Vulcan B Mk.1 XH502

Delivered in November 1958 and fitted with Olympus 104 engines. Converted to B.1A standard in 1962. **Served with:** 617 Squadron, 50 Squadron and Waddington Wing. This image taken on Christmas Island, Pacific during a visit by three Vulcans in 1959. Flown to Scampton in January 1968 for instructional duties, then returned to Waddington for fire fighting.

Vulcan B Mk.1 XH503

Delivered in December 1958 and fitted with Olympus 104 engines. Converted to B.1A standard in 1963.
Served with: 83 Squadron, 44 Squadron and Waddington Wing. Transferred to St. Athan on 6 December 1966 and sold as scrap on 8 November 1968

Peter Middlebrook

Vulcan B Mk.1 XH504

Delivered in March 1959 and fitted with Olympus 104 engines. Converted to B.1A standard in 1961. **Served with:** 230 OCU and Waddington Wing. Transferred to Cottesmore fire dump on 4 January 1968 and later scrapped.

Vulcan B Mk.1 XH505

Delivered in March 1959 and fitted with Olympus 104 engines. Converted to B.1A standard in 1960. **Served with:** 230 OCU, 617 Squadron, 50 Squadron and Waddington Wing. Delivered to Finningley fire dump on 9 January 1968 and later scrapped.

Gordon 'Mac' McMurray

Vulcan B Mk.1 XH506

Delivered in April 1959 and fitted with Olympus 104 engines. Converted to B.1A standard in 1960. Appeared in the James Bond film Thunderball (1965).
Served with: 44 Squadron, 101 Squadron, 617 Squadron, 50 Squadron and Waddington Wing. Withdrawn from service on 10 January 1968 at 19 MU, St Athan and sold as scrap to Bradbury & Co.

XH

Vulcan B Mk.1 XH532

Delivered in March 1959 and fitted with Olympus 104 engines. **This aircraft was the 45th and last B.1 produced.** Installation of Yellow Sun and tests at RAE Farnborough. Converted to B.1A standard in 1962. **Served with:** 230 OCU, 101 Squadron and Waddington Wing. Delivered to St. Athan on 17 May 1966 and sold as scrap on 8 November 1968.

Vulcan B Mk.2 XH533

First Flight on 19 August 1958. Fitted with Olympus 200 engines (small intakes), but retained Mk.1 tailcone. **First production B.2. Served with:** MoS Air Fleet at Woodford for Contractor's trials until 26 March 1959. Further trials continued at A&AEE, A.V. Roe and Hawker Siddeley. Moved to St. Athan for storage in October 1967 and finally allocated for instructional use as No. (8048M) and sold as scrap on 15 October 1970.

Vulcan B Mk.2 XH534

Completed in July 1959 and fitted with Olympus 201 engines (small intakes). Used in a wide range of Manufacturer's and A&AEE trials between 1959 and 1965. Moved to 230 OCU in December 1966 and transferred to Manufacturer for storage in April 1972. Converted to B.2 (MRR) in August 1973. **Served with:** 27 Squadron from August 1974 and moved to St. Athan in August 1981. Sold as scrap on 18 February 1982 to Harold John & Co.

Vulcan B Mk.2 XH535

Completed in May 1960 and fitted with Olympus 201 engines (small intakes). **Served with:** A&AEE for flight trials. Moved to Woodford for preparation prior to EMC tests in Douglas, USA for Skybolt installation. Crashed at Chute, west of Boscombe Down, on 11 May 1964 after entering an uncontrollable spin whilst Avro test pilot was attempting very low speed flying. Pilot and co-pilot ejected, rear crew were unable to escape due to g-forces.

Peter Middlebrook

Malcolm Taylor Collection © Geoff Parrish

Fred Martin

Vulcan B Mk.2 XH536

Completed in July 1959 and fitted with Olympus 201 engines (small intakes) and initially the Mk.1 tailcone. From December 1959 to September 1963 used on Radio and navigation equipment trials at A V Roe and A&AEE. Also installation of Heading Reference System (HRS) and roller map trials. **Served with:** 9, 12 and 35 Squadrons. Involved in a flying accident on 11 February 1966 near Clwyth, Brecon Beacons during low-level exercise, all crew killed.

Peter March Collection

Vulcan B Mk.2 XH537

Completed in August 1959 and fitted with Olympus 201 engines (small intakes) and initially the Mk.1 tailcone. Employed on numerous trials at MoS Air Fleet, RAE Farnborough, A&AEE for armament trials. Allocated for Skybolt and flown with dummy missiles. Converted to B.2 (MMR) February 1978. **Served with:** 230 OCU and 27 Squadron. Transferred to Abingdon in March 1982 as instructional airframe No.(8749M) and scrapped in 1991. The cockpit section survives at the Bournemouth Aviation Museum.

Vulcan B Mk.2 XH538

Completed in September 1959 and fitted with Olympus 201 engines (small intakes) and initially the Mk.1 tailcone. Manufacturers and A&AEE trials until January 1961. Used for Blue Steel and Skybolt trials. Scampton Wing until May 1969 and Waddington Wing until April 1970. **Served with:** 230 OCU, 27 Squadron, 35 Squadron, IX, 44, 50 and 101 Squadrons. Transferred to St. Athan in March 1981 and sold as scrap to W. Harold & Co. on 31 August 1981.

BAE Systems

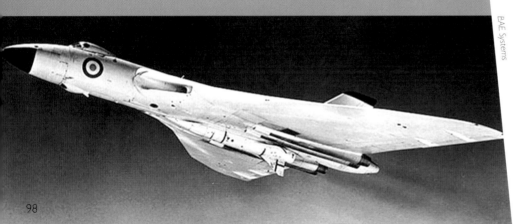

Vulcan B Mk.2 XH539

Completed in September 1959 and fitted with Olympus 201 engines (small intakes). Despatched to Edinburgh Field, Australia for the first live firing of Blue Steel at Woomera. In 1964 involved in High all-up weight and bomb bay tank tests including 2 engine take-offs. In 1969 to A&AEE for trials of conventional armament for low-level role. Withdrawn from use in December 1971 and moved to Waddington fire dump in March 1972.

Vulcan B Mk.2 **XH554**

Completed in October 1959 and fitted with Olympus 201 engines (small intakes). **Served with:** 83 Squadron and 230 OCU. Return to A V Roe for retrofit March 1963, including enlarged intakes. Flying accident Cat. 3R September 1973, repaired on site. Moved to Fire Fighting School Catterick on 9 June 1981 as No.(8694M).

Vulcan B Mk.2 **XH555**

Completed in June 1961 and fitted with Olympus 201 engines (small intakes). **Served with:** 27 Squadron and 230 OCU. Heavy landing at Finningley in 1968, airframe then used for fatigue destruction tests at HSA Woodford until 1970. Struck off charge in 1971 and scrapped in 1977.

Vulcan B Mk.2 **XH556**

Completed in September 1961 and fitted with Olympus 201 engines and the last B2 to be fitted with the early shallow engine intakes. **Served with:** 27 Squadron and 230 OCU. Struck off charge following an undercarriage collapse at RAF Finningley on 4 April 1966 and moved to the fire dump. Later scrapped.

Vulcan B Mk.2 **XH557**

Completed in May 1960 and initially fitted with Olympus 201/301 engines. Moved to Bristol Siddeley for engine trials on 21 June 1960. Fitted with Mk. 301 engines in outer nacelles, later fitted with four 301s. First B2 with enlarged intakes. **Served with:** Cottesmore Wing, Waddington Wing, Akrotiri Wing and 50 Squadron. Sold to the Bird Group as scrap in December 1982.

APN

Malcolm Taylor Collection © Hubert Parrish

Fred Martin

Terry Senior

Fred Martin

Vulcan B Mk.2 XH558

Completed on 30 June 1960 and fitted with Olympus 201 engines. **Served with:** 230 OCU July 1960 (first B2 to enter RAF service) at Waddington, then June 1961 to December 1968 at RAF Finningley. Conversion to B.2 (MRR) in August 1973, 230 OCU October 1976, 27 Squadron November 1976, Waddington Wing March 1982. Conversion to K.2 July 1982, 50 Squadron October 1982. Waddington Station Flight April 1984. Marham Display September 1984, Waddington Display November 1984. Conversion to B.2 April 1985. Moved to 55 Squadron September 1985. Last Vulcan in RAF service. Sold to C. Walton and delivered to Bruntingthorpe on 23 March 1993 and struck off charge. Registered G-VLCN. Sold to Vulcan to the Sky Trust and restored to flight in October 2007.

Vulcan B Mk.2 XH559

Completed in July 1960 and fitted with Olympus 201 engines. **Served with:** 230 OCU from August 1960. Move to A V Roe for Major Servicing and modifications. Returned to 230 OCU in May 1965. HSAL Mods August 1968 again returning to 230 OCU February 1970. Transferred to St. Athan in May 1981 and sold as scrap to Harold John & Co. on 29 January 1982.

Vulcan B Mk.2 XH560

Completed in September 1960 and fitted with Olympus 201 engines. **Served with:** 230 OCU from October 1960, to Woodford to investigate 4 engine flame-out November 1960. Allocated for Skybolt Development and Mods May 1961, returning to 12 Squadron in September 1962. 230 OCU November 1962, Cottesmore Wing August 1965 (IX, 12 and 35 Squadrons), Waddington Wing April 1967, Cottesmore Wing June 1967. Conversion to B.2(MRR) role February 1973, 27 Squadron March 1974, Waddington March 1982 (IX, 44, 50 and 101 Squadrons). Converted to K.2 in July 1982 returning to 44 and 50 Squadrons Waddington. Station Flight Waddington April 1984 and Marham August 1984. Struck off charge Cat 5(c) January 1985, nose saved for restoration.

Vulcan B Mk.2 XH561

Completed in October 1960 and fitted with Olympus 201 engines. **Served with:** 230 OCU November 1960,

Waddington Wing August 1967, Cottesmore Wing May 1968, Akrotiri Wing March 1969, 35 Squadron March 1975, 50 Squadron September 1981. Conversion to K.2 May 1982, 50 Squadron June 1982, Waddington Station Flight April 1984. Struck off charge for fire fighting at RAF Catterick, allocated No.(8809M).

Vulcan B Mk.2 XH562

Completed in November 1960 and fitted with Olympus 201 engines. **Served with:** 230 OCU December 1960, 35 Squadron, March 1963, 230 OCU September 1963, Cottesmore Wing August 1965, 50 Squadron March 1966, Waddington Wing February 1967, Cottesmore Wing April 1968, Akrotiri Wing January 1969, Waddington Wing May 1975, 230 OCU September 1977, 35 Squadron December 1980, IX Squadron July 1981, 101 Squadron June 1982. Moved to Fire Fighting School RAF Catterick August 1982. Allocated No.(8758M). Scrapped 1984.

Vulcan B Mk.2 XH563

Completed in December 1960 and fitted with Olympus 201 engines. **Served with:** 83 Squadron December 1960, 12 Squadron November 1962, 230 OCU March 1965, Waddington Wing August 1968, 230 OCU March 1969, Scampton Wing May 1971, 230 OCU May 1971, Conversion to B.2 (MRR) February 1973. 27 Squadron December 1973. Allocated No. (8744M) March 1982 for preservation at Scampton. Later Scrapped.

Avro Vulcan XJ serials

Vulcan B Mk.2 XJ780

Completed on 10 January 1961 and fitted with Olympus 201 engines. **Served with:** 83 Squadron January 1961, 12 Squadron November 1962, 230 OCU August 1963, Waddington Wing October 1967, Cottesmore Wing December 1968, Waddington Wing April 1969, Akrotiri Wing January 1970, Waddington Wing January 1975. Modification to B.2 (MRR) Std. March 1976. 27 Squadron November 1976. Allocated for spares recovery in March 1982. Sold to Bird Group as scrap in November 1982.

Fred Martin

H John Black

Vulcan B Mk.2 **XJ781**

Completed in February 1961 and fitted with Olympus 201 engines. **Served with:** 83 Squadron February 1961, 12 Squadron October 1962, 230 OCU February 1964, Waddington Wing February 1966, Cottesmore Wing April 1968 and Akrotiri Wing April 1969. Damaged on 23 May 1973 during landing at Shiraz, Iran, swung off runway into gully. Struck off charge on 27 May 1973.

Vulcan B Mk.2 **XJ782**

Completed in February 1961 and fitted with Olympus 201 engines. **Served with:** 83 Squadron February 1961, 12 Squadron October 1962, 230 OCU December 1963, Waddington Wing March 1966, Cottesmore Wing April 1968, Akrotiri Wing March 1969 and Waddington Wing January 1975. Modified to B.2(MRR) standard January 1977. Moved to 27 Squadron February 1977. Flew last Vulcan sortie at Scampton on 31 March 1982. Allocated to Scampton dump on 31 March 1982 but re-allocated to 101 Squadron in May 1982. To RAF Finningley for gate display on 4 September 1982 as No.(8766M). Later transferred to dump and scrapped.

Vulcan B Mk.2 **XJ783**

Completed on 6 March 1961 and fitted with Olympus 201 engines. **Served with:** 83 Squadron March 1961, IX Squadron November 1962, 230 OCU February 1964, Waddington Wing January 1966, Cottesmore Wing March 1968, Akrotiri Wing January 1969, 35 Squadron January 1975, 230 OCU August 1976, 35 Squadron August 1976, 617 Squadron November 1978 and 35 Squadron April 1981. Used as spares recovery from March 1982 and sold to the Bird Group as scrap in November 1982.

Vulcan B Mk.2 **XJ784**

Completed on 30 March 1961 and fitted with Olympus 201 engines, but later updated by Gloster Aircraft, Morton Valence to T1 of Olympus 301. Used by Woodford for handling trials. To A&AEE March 1961 for rapid take-off equipment fitting. **Served with:** 230 OCU December 1966, Akrotiri Wing July 1970, Waddington Wing January 1975, IX Squadron February 1972, 44 Squadron July 1979 and 101 Squadron June 1980. Used as spares recovery September 1982 and sold to the Bird Group as scrap on 8 December 1982.

Vulcan B Mk.2 **XJ823**

Completed on 20 April 1961 and fitted with Olympus 201 engines. **Served with:** 27 Squadron April 1961, 35 Squadron January 1963, Cottesmore Wing March 1964, 230 OCU May 1964. Waddington Wing November 1966, Cottesmore Wing April 1968, Akrotiri Wing February 1969, Waddington Wing January 1975, IX Squadron February 1975. Modified to B.2 (MRR) standard March 1977. 27 Squadron April 1977, 35 Squadron April 1981, Waddington Wing March 1982, IX Squadron March 1982, 50 Squadron April 1982. Sold to T. Stoddart on 21 January 1983. Delivered to Solway Aviation Society Carlisle on 24 January 1983.

Vulcan B Mk.2 **XJ824**

Completed on 11 May 1961 and fitted with Olympus 201 engines. **Served with:** 27 Squadron May 1961, IX Squadron February 1963, 230 OCU December 1963, Cottesmore Wing July 1966, Waddington Wing October 1966, Cottesmore Wing July 1968, Akrotiri Wing February 1969, 35 Squadron January 1975, 230 OCU February 1977, 44 Squadron October 1979, 101 Squadron July 1982. Last Vulcan to leave Bitteswell after manufacturers modifications on 8 July 1981. Delivered to Imperial War Museum Duxford on 13 March 1982.

Vulcan B Mk.2 **XJ825**

Completed on 27 July 1961 and fitted with Olympus 201 engines. **Served with:** 27 Squadron July 1961, 35 Squadron February 1963, 230 OCU April 1964, Cottesmore Wing September 1965, Waddington Wing April 1967, Cottesmore Wing February 1968, Akrotiri Wing February 1969, 35 Squadron January 1975, Modified to B2 (MRR) standard January 1976, 27 Squadron December 1976, 35 Squadron April 1981, 101 Squadron March 1982. Conversion to K.2 May 1982. To 50 Squadron July 1982. Allocated No.(8810M) battle damage repair duties. Struck off charge April 1984 and scrapped in 1992.

SURVIVOR

SURVIVOR

XJ

Avro Vulcan XL serials

Vulcan B Mk.2 **XL317**

Completed on 14 July 1961 and fitted with Olympus 201
engines. To MoA Air Fleet for Blue Steel modifications
July 1961, first airframe to be modified. Remodified to
conventional bombing role in 1971. **Served with:** 617
Squadron July 1962, 230 OCU April 1974, 617 Squadron
May 1974, To Akrotiri as No.(8725M) for crash rescue
training December 1981. Scrapped December 1986.

Vulcan B Mk.2 **XL318**

Completed on 30 August 1961 and fitted with Olympus
201 engines. Blue Steel modifications. **Served with:**
617 Squadron September 1961, 230 OCU May 1972,
27 Squadron January 1974, 230 OCU February 1974,
Waddington Wing June 1975, 230 OCU August 1975,
Waddington Wing November 1979, 230 OCU February
1980, 617 Squadron July 1981. Last Sortie by a 617
Squadron Vulcan on 11 December 1981. Assigned to RAF
Museum on 4 January 1982 as No.(8733M). Transported to
Hendon on 12 February 1982.

SURVIVOR

Vulcan B Mk.2 **XL319**

Completed on 19 October 1961 and fitted with Olympus
201 engines. Blue Steel Modifications. **Served with:** 617
Squadron October 1961, 230 OCU May 1970, Scampton
Wing November 1970, 617 Squadron April 1971, 230
OCU September 1972, 35 Squadron October 1978,
44 Squadron March 1982. Sold to North Eastern Aircraft
Museum on 20 January 1983. Delivered to Sunderland on
21 January 1983.

SURVIVOR

Vulcan B Mk.2 **XL320**

Completed on 30 November 1961 and fitted with
Olympus 201 engines. Blue Steel Modifications. **Served
with:** 617 Squadron December 1961, 83 Squadron July
1971, 27 Squadron September 1971, 230 OCU March
1972, Delivered to St. Athan on 2 July 1981. Sold to W.
Harold & Co. on 31 August 1981 as scrap.

Vulcan B Mk.2 **XL321**

Completed on 10 January 1962 and fitted with Olympus 201 engines. Blue Steel Modifications. **Served with:** 617 Squadron January 1962, 27 Squadron January 1971, 230 OCU October 1972, 617 Squadron April 1973, 44 Squadron July 1976, 230 OCU November 1976, 35 Squadron July 1981, 617 Squadron September 1981, 35 Squadron October 1981, 50 Squadron January 1982. Delivered to Fire Fighting School Catterick on 19 August 1982 as No.(8759M). Highest individual Vulcan operational flying hours (6,952). Scrapped in 1987.

Vulcan B Mk.2 **XL359**

Completed on 31 January 1961 and fitted with Olympus 201 engines. Blue Steel Modifications. **Served with:** 617 Squadron February 1962, 27 Squadron March 1971, 230 OCU October 1971, 35 Squadron July 1981. Allocated as Gate Guard at RAF Scampton (provisionally 8744M), replaced by XH563. Sold to the Bird Group as scrap in November 1982.

Vulcan B.Mk.2 **XL360**

Completed on 28 February 1962 and fitted with Olympus 201 engines. Blue Steel Modifications. **Served with:** 617 Squadron March 1962, 230 OCU July 1971, Waddington Wing August 1975, 230 OCU October 1975, 617 Squadron December 1977, 35 Squadron May 1978, 101 Squadron January 1982. Sold to Midland Air Museum on 26 January 1983 and delivered to Baginton on 4 February 1983.

SURVIVOR

Fred Martin

Vulcan B Mk.2 **XL361**

Completed on 14 March 1962 and fitted with Olympus 201 engines. Blue Steel Modified. **Served with:** 617 Squadron March 1962, 230 OCU October 1970, Scampton Wing November 1970, 230 OCU November 1970, Scampton Wing April 1971, 27 Squadron/230 OCU January 1974, A&AEE August 1975, 617 Squadron September 1975, 35 Squadron August 1977, IX Squadron April 1981. Accident at Goose Bay, Canada on 13 November 1981. Declared Cat 5 and gifted to Happy Valley, Goose Bay for display.

SURVIVOR

XL

Vulcan B Mk.2 **XL384**

Completed on 30 March 1962 and fitted with Olympus 201 engines. Blue Steel Modified. **Served with:** 230 OCU April 1962, Scampton Wing August 1964, Waddington Wing March 1970, 230 OCU November 1970. Suffered a heavy landing on 12 August 1971. Allocated No.(8505M) on 30 September 1976 as escape trainer. Later transferred to crash rescue training as No.(8670M) and struck off charge on 23 May 1985.

Vulcan B Mk.2 **XL385**

Completed on 17 April 1962 and fitted with Olympus 301 engines. Blue Steel modified. **Served with:** IX Squadron April 1962, Scampton Wing October 1964. Two engines exploded 6 April 1967 at RAF Scampton as pilot throttled up for take-off. Crew abandoned aircraft which was destroyed by fire. Parts from the engine turbine discs found 500 yards away. Struck off charge on 7 April 1967.

Vulcan B Mk.2 **XL386**

Completed on 11 May 1962 and fitted with Olympus 301 engines. Blue Steel Modified. **Served with:** IX Squadron May 1962, Scampton Wing August 1965, 230 OCU April 1970, 44 Squadron September 1977, 101 Squadron May 1981. Delivered to Central Training Establishment at RAF Manston on 26 August 1982 for crash rescue training as No.(8760M). Blown-up in September 1992.

Vulcan B Mk.2 **XL387**

Completed on 31 May 1962 and fitted with Olympus 301 engines. Blue Steel modified. **Served with:** 230 OCU June 1962, Scampton Wing February 1965, 230 OCU July 1972, 101 Squadron January 1973, 50 Squadron August 1975. Transferred to St. Athan for crash rescue training on 28 January 1982. Allotted No.(8748M). Sold to T. Bradbury as scrap on 2 July 1983.

XL

Vulcan B Mk.2 **XL388**

Completed on 13 June 1962 and fitted with Olympus 301 engines. Blue Steel Modified. **Served with:** IX Squadron June 1962, (Coningsby Wing), 230 OCU April 1971, 617 Squadron September 1972, 230 OCU September 1972, 617 Squadron February 1973, 230 OCU May 1973, 617 Squadron November 1973, 230 OCU March 1974, 44 Squadron April 1974. To Honington fire dump on 2 April 1982 as No.(8750M). Sold to Swefeling Group as scrap on 13 June 1985.

Vulcan B Mk.2 **XL389**

Completed on 11 July 1962 and fitted with Olympus 301 engines. Blue Steel Modified. **Served with:** 230 OCU July 1962, Scampton Wing May 1965, 230 OCU November 1970, 617 Squadron December 1970, 230 OCU April 1972, 617 Squadron June 1972, 230 OCU January 1973, 617 Squadron January 1973, IX Squadron June 1974, 44 Squadron July 1979, 101 Squadron June 1980. To St. Athan on 6 April 1981. Sold as scrap to W. Harold on 31 August 1981.

Vulcan B Mk.2 **XL390**

Completed on 19 July 1962 and fitted with Olympus 301 engines. Blue Steel Modified. First production aircraft with Skybolt hardpoints. **Served with:** IX Squadron July 1962, Scampton Wing May 1965, 230 OCU April 1971, 617 Squadron June 1971, 230 OCU May 1974 and 617 Squadron June 1974. Crashed during practice for air display at Glenview NAS, USA on 12 August 1978.

Vulcan B Mk.2 **XL391**

Completed on 22 May 1963 and fitted with Olympus 301 engines. Blue Steel Modified. A&AEE May 1963, BCDU June 1965, A&AEE January 1966. **Served with:** Cottesmore Wing July 1968, Akrotiri Wing February 1969, IX Squadron January 1975, 101 Squadron June 1980. Selected for 'Black Buck' modifications, but not used operationally. 44 Squadron June 1982. Sold to Manchester Vulcan Bomber Society on 11 February 1983. Delivered to Blackpool on 16 February 1983. Scrapped in 2006 after attempt to sell on eBay.

Chris England

Fred Martin

Vulcan B Mk.2 **XL392**

Completed on 31 July 1962 and fitted with Olympus 201 engines. Blue Steel Modified. **Served with:** 83 Squadron August 1962, 230 OCU December 1970, Scampton Wing December 1970, 230 OCU January 1973, 617 Squadron January 1973, 35 Squadron January 1982. Delivered to RAF Valley for crash rescue training as No.(8745M) on 24 March 1982. Later scrapped.

Vulcan B Mk.2 **XL425**

Completed on 30 August 1962 and fitted with Olympus 201 engines. Blue Steel Modified. **Served with:** 83 Squadron August 1962, Scampton Wing March 1966, 617 Squadron November 1972, 27 Squadron November 1973, 617 Squadron April 1974. Assessed as Cat.5 (scrap) at RAF Scampton on 4 January 1982. Sold to Bird Group as scrap during April 1982

Vulcan B Mk.2 **XL426**

Completed on 7 September 1962 and fitted with Olympus 201 engines. Blue Steel modified. **Served with:** 83 Squadron September 1962, (Scampton Wing), 230 OCU March 1972, 617 Squadron April 1972, 230 OCU, 617 and 72 Squadrons in 1972 and 230 OCU and 617 Squadron in 1973. 27 and 617 Squadrons in 1974. 50 Squadron January 1982, 55 Squadron April 1984, Station Flight Waddington (for Display Flight). Sold to Roy Jacobson and delivered to Southend on 19 December 1986. Registered as G-VJET. Sold to the Vulcan Restoration Trust in 1993 and maintained in taxiing condition.

Terry Senior

SURVIVOR

Vulcan B Mk.2 **XL427**

Completed on 29 September 1962 and fitted with Olympus 201 engines. Blue Steel modified. **Served with:** 83 Squadron October 1962 (Scampton Wing), 617 Squadron September 1969, 27 Squadron March 1971, 230 OCU June 1972, 617 Squadron July 1972, 230 OCU September 1972, 27 Squadron January 1974, 230 OCU August 1976, IX Squadron May 1977, 50 Squadron April 1981, IX Squadron October 1981, 44 Squadron June 1982. Delivered to Macrihanish, Scotland for crash rescue training on 13 August 1982 as No.(8756M). Scrapped 1986.

XL

Vulcan B Mk.2 XL443

Completed on 4 October 1962 and fitted with Olympus 201 engines. Blue Steel modified. **Served with:** 83 Squadron October 1962, Scampton Wing, Akrotiri Wing April 1972, 35 Squadron January 1975. Allocated to RAF Museum on 4 January 1982 but not taken up. Later sold to Bird Group as scrap in April 1982.

Vulcan B Mk.2 XL444

Completed on 29 October 1962 and fitted with Olympus 201 engines. Blue Steel modified. **Served with:** 27 Squadron November 1962 Scampton Wing, 230 OCU June 1966, Scampton Wing June 1967, 230 OCU April 1971, 27 Squadron May 1971, 617 Squadron September 1971, 230/617 Squadron July 1972, 617 Squadron December 1973, 35 Squadron May 1978, IX Squadron April 1981. Aircraft assigned Cat.5(c) at RAF Waddington and grounded on 10 September 1982. Sold to Bird Group as scrap on 8 December 1982.

Vulcan B Mk.2 XL445

Completed on 19 November 1962 and fitted with Olympus 201 engines. Blue Steel modified. **Served with:** 27 Squadron November 1962 Scampton Wing, Waddington Wing September 1966, Cottesmore Wing April 1968, Akrotiri Wing January 1969, 35 Squadron January 1975, Waddington Wing June 1977, 35 Squadron October 1977, 230 OCU October 1978, 35 Squadron July 1981, 44 Squadron November 1981. Conversion to K.2 May 1982. 50 Squadron July 1982. Allocated No.(8811M) on 22 March 1984 for battle damage repair and crash rescue training. Delivered to Lyneham on 1 April 1984. Later scrapped.

Vulcan B Mk.2 XL446

Completed on 19 November 1962 and fitted with Olympus 201 engines. Blue Steel modified. **Served with:** 27 Squadron November 1962 Scampton Wing, Waddington Wing September 1966, 230 OCU December 1967, Scampton Wing April 1972, Akrotiri Wing July 1972, 35 Squadron January 1975, Waddington Wing May 1978, 617 Squadron October 1978, 35 Squadron January 1982. Grounded on 1 March 1982 and sold to Bird Group as scrap in November 1982.

Avro Vulcan XM serials

Vulcan B Mk.2 XM569

Completed on 4 January 1963, fitted with Olympus 201 engines and Blue Steel modified. **Served with:** 27 Squadron February 1963 Scampton Wing, Waddington Wing November 1966, Cottesmore Wing January 1968, Akrotiri Wing February 1969, 27 Squadron July 1974, IX Squadron November 1976, 50 Squadron June 1979, 101 Squadron September 1981, 44 Squadron August 1982. Sold to Wales Aircraft Museum on 21 January 1983 and delivered to Cardiff on 2 February 1983. The main airframe was later scrapped but the nose section is currently on view at the Flying Shack, Staverton Airport.

Vulcan B Mk.2 XM570

Completed on 26 February 1963 with Olympus 201 engines. Blue Steel modified. **Served with:** 27 Squadron February 1963 Scampton Wing, Waddington Wing January 1967, Cottesmore Wing January 1968, Akrotiri Wing February 1969, 27 Squadron March 1974, 35 Squadron December 1976, 230 OCU February 1977, 35 Squadron March 1977, 617 Squadron September 1978, 35 Squadron October 1978. Delivered to St. Athan March 1981 and sold to Harold John & Co. as scrap on 29 January 1982.

Vulcan B Mk.2 XM571

Completed on 20 February 1963 with Olympus 201 engines. Blue Steel modified. **Served with:** 83 Squadron February 1963 Scampton Wing, Cottesmore Wing January 1967, Waddington Wing July 1967, Cottesmore Wing September 1967, Waddington Wing December 1967, Akrotiri Wing March 1969, 27 Squadron January 1975, 35 Squadron April 1975, Waddington Wing June 1975, 35 Squadron November 1975, 50 Squadron June 1976, 35 Squadron November 1976, St. Athan January 1979, 617 Squadron March 1979, Waddington Wing August 1979, 617 Squadron December 1979, 101 Squadron January 1982. Converted to K.2 May 1982. 50 Squadron August 1982, Waddington Station Flight April 1984. Allocated No. (8812M) March 1984. Delivered to Gibraltar for preservation on 9 May 1984. Later scrapped.

Vulcan B Mk.2 **XM572**

Completed on 28 February 1963 with Olympus 201 engines. Blue Steel modified. **Served with:** 83 Squadron February 1963 Scampton Wing, Cottesmore Wing April 1968, Akrotiri Wing March 1969, 35 Squadron January 1975, IX Squadron September 1981. Grounded on 10 September 1982 and sold to the Bird Group as scrap on 30 November 1982.

Vulcan B Mk.2 **XM573**

Completed on 26 March 1963 with Olympus 201 engines. Blue Steel modified. **Served with:** 83 Squadron March 1963 Scampton Wing, Waddington Wing April 1967, 230 OCU February 1968, Akrotiri Wing June 1970, 27 Squadron April 1974, 44 Squadron March 1977, 230 OCU December 1978, IX Squadron April 1981 Scampton Wing May 1982. Delivered to Offutt AFB, USA on 7 June 1982 and presented to the USAF on 12 June 1982.

SURVIVOR

Vulcan B Mk.2 **XM574**

Completed on 12 June 1963 with Olympus 301 engines. Blue Steel modified. **Served with:** 27 Squadron June 1963 Scampton Wing, 230 OCU May 1971, 27 Squadron May 1971, 101 Squadron November 1971, Akrotiri Wing August 1973, 35 Squadron January 1975, 617 Squadron August 1975. To St. Athan on 31 August 1981 and sold to Harold John & Co. as scrap on 29 January 1982.

Vulcan B Mk.2 **XM575**

Completed on 21 May 1963 with Olympus 301 engines. Blue Steel modified. **Served with:** 617 Squadron May 1963, Waddington Wing July 1970, Scampton Wing November 1970, 230 OCU May 1971, 617 Squadron May 1971, 101 Squadron March 1974, 50 Squadron June 1978 and 44 Squadron August 1979. Sold to Leicester Air Museum on 25 January 1983. Registration G-BLMC was reserved in August 1984 for a possible ferry flight to Bruntingthorpe but was never taken up. Flown to East Midlands Airport Aeropark on 28 January 1983.

SURVIVOR

Geoff Gaukrodger

SURVIVOR   Andy Leitch

Vulcan B Mk.2 **XM576**

Completed on 14 June 1963 with Olympus 301 engines.
Blue Steel modified. **Served with:** Scampton Wing, from
21 June 1963. Crash landed at Scampton on 25 May
1965 during asymmetric approach. Wing hit ground on
overshoot, aircraft swung and hit the control tower, all crew
survived. Assessed for repair as Cat 4 but reclassified as
Cat.5(c) and struck off charge on 7 December 1965.

Vulcan B Mk.2 **XM594**

Completed on 9 July 1963 with Olympus 301 engines.
Blue Steel modified. **Served with:** 27 Squadron July
1963 Scampton Wing, Waddington Wing August 1972,
101 Squadron June 1975, 44 Squadron May 1977. Sold to
Newark Air Museum on 19 January 1983 and delivered to
Winthorpe on 7 February 1983.

Vulcan B Mk.2 **XM595**

Completed on 21 August 1963 with Olympus 301 engines.
Blue Steel modified. **Served with:** 617 Squadron August
1963 Scampton Wing, 27 Squadron August 1974, 617
Squadron September 1975, 35 Squadron November 1976,
617 Squadron February 1978 and 35 Squadron January
1982. Grounded on 1 March 1982 and sold to Bird Group
as scrap in November 1982.

Vulcan B Mk.2 **XM596**

Aircraft not completed. Withdrawn from the production line
in 1963 and installed on the test rig at Woodford to simulate
future low level flying operations as the fleet's Fatigue Test
Specimen. The airframe never wore its allotted serial
number. Scrapped in 1972.

Vulcan B Mk.2 **XM597**

Completed on 26 August 1963 with Olympus 301 engines.
Blue Steel modified. **Served with:** 12 Squadron August
1963 Coningsby Wing, Cottesmore Wing December 1964,
Waddington Wing April 1968, A&AEE November 1971,
101 Squadron August 1973, 44 Squadron September 1975,
50 Squadron April 1976, IX Squadron May 1979,
44 Squadron October 1981, 101 Squadron July 1982.

Modified for 'Black Buck' operations. 44 Squadron July 1982, 50 Squadron December 1982. Delivered to Royal Scottish Museum of Flight, East Fortune on 12 April 1984.

Vulcan B Mk.2 **XM598**

Completed on 30 August 1963 with Olympus 301 engines. **Served with:** 12 Squadron September 1963 Coningsby Wing, Cottesmore Wing November 1964, Waddington Wing April 1968, 101 Squadron May 1972, 44 Squadron August 1975, 50 Squadron April 1978, IX Squadron October 1979, 50 Squadron April 1971, 44 Squadron June 1982. Modified for 'Black Buck' operations. Allocated No.(8778M) on 4 January 1983 and delivered to RAF Cosford Aerospace Museum on 20 January 1983.

Vulcan B Mk.2 **XM599**

Completed on 30 September 1963 with Olympus 301 engines. **Served with:** 35 Squadron October 1963 Coningsby Wing, Waddington Wing December 1968, 101 Squadron May 1972, 50 Squadron March 1977, 44 Squadron June 1979. Delivered to St. Athan on 27 May 1981. Sold to H. John & Co. as scrap on 29 January 1982.

Vulcan B Mk.2 **XM600**

Completed on 30 September 1963 with Olympus 301 engines. **Served with:** 35 Squadron Coningsby Wing October 1963, Waddington Wing May 1968, 101 Squadron August 1973. Aircraft crashed on 17 January 1977 near Spilsby, Lincs following an engine bay fire, crew escaped successfully. Struck off charge on 18 January 1977.

Vulcan B Mk.2 **XM601**

Completed on 31 October 1963 with Olympus 301 engines. **Served with:** IX Squadron October 1963 Coningsby Wing. Crashed during overshoot from asymmetric approach to Coningsby on 7 October 1964, crew killed. Struck off charge on 8 October 1964.

XM

Vulcan B Mk.2 **XM602**

Completed on 11 November 1963 with Olympus 301 engines. **Served with:** 12 Squadron November 1963, Cottesmore Wing June 1965, Waddington Wing April 1968, IX Squadron December 1975, 230 OCU October 1976, 35 Squadron October 1976, Waddington Wing November 1976, 101 Squadron May 1980. To St. Athan on 7 January 1982. Transferred to St. Athan Historic Aircraft Museum on 16 March as No.(8771M). Scrapped in 1993, with nose section preserved by Avro Heritage Society.

Vulcan B Mk.2 **XM603**

Completed on 29 November 1963 with Olympus 301 engines. **Served with:** IX Squadron December 1963, Cottesmore Wing June 1965, Waddington Wing April 1968, Coningsby Wing, Cottesmore Wing and Waddington Wing January 1968, 50 Squadron August 1975, 101 Squadron December 1980, 44 Squadron July 1981. Sold to British Aerospace for preservation, delivered to Woodford on 12 March 1982. Mock-up aircraft for K.2 conversions.

Vulcan B Mk.2 **XM604**

Completed on 29 November 1963 with Olympus 301 engines. **Served with:** 35 Squadron December 1963, Coningsby Wing, Cottesmore Wing. Crashed near Cottesmore on 30 January 1968 following engine failure and loss of control at low altitude. Pilot and co-pilot ejected (pilot whilst aircraft was inverted, saved by his undeveloped parachute catching on power cables), rear crew killed. Struck off charge on 31 January 1968.

Vulcan B Mk.2 **XM605**

Completed on 17 December 1963 with Olympus 301 engines. **Served with:** IX Squadron December 1963, Coningsby Wing, Cottesmore Wing and Waddington Wing December 1968, 101 Squadron September 1973, 50 Squadron May 1979. Delivered to Castle AFB, USA on 2 September 1981. Presented to USAF on 8 September 1981.

Vulcan B Mk.2 **XM606**

Completed on 18 December 1963 with Olympus 301 engines. **Served with:** 12 Squadron December 1963, Coningsby Wing, Cottesmore Wing February 1965, MoA loan for TFR development trials June 1965. Cottesmore Wing April 1968, Waddington Wing May 1968, 101 Squadron December 1975, IX Squadron June 1979. Delivered to Barksdale AFB, USA on 7 June 1982. Presented to USAF on 14 June 1983.

Vulcan B Mk.2 **XM607**

Completed on 30 December 1963 with Olympus 301 engines. **Served with:** 35 Squadron January 1964, Cottesmore Wing, Waddington Wing May 1968, 44 Squadron April 1976, IX Squadron May 1979, 101 Squadron March 1981, 44 Squadron July 1981, Modified for 'Black Buck' operations and flew the first mission on 30 April 1982. 44 Squadron June 1982. Withdrawn from use on 17 December 1982 and allocated No.(8779M). To static display at RAF Waddington on 19 January 1983.

Vulcan B Mk.2 **XM608**

Completed on 28 January 1964 with Olympus 301 engines. **Served with:** IX Squadron January 1964, Cottesmore Wing April 1965, Waddington Wing February 1968, 50 Squadron April 1975. Moved to St. Athan on 6 April 1981 for spares recovery. Sold to Bird Group as scrap on 2 December 1982.

Vulcan B Mk.2 **XM609**

Completed on 28 January 1964 with Olympus 301 engines. **Served with:** 12 Squadron January 1964, Cottesmore Wing March 1965, 230 OCU August 1967, Cottesmore Wing October 1967, Waddington Wing March 1968, IX Squadron September 1975, 44 Squadron April 1976. To St. Athan on 12 March 1981. Sold to W. Harold & Co. as scrap on 31 August 1981.

XM

Michael Slorance

Vulcan B Mk.2 **XM610**

Completed on 10 February 1964 with Olympus 301
engines. **Served with:** IX Squadron February 1964,
Cottesmore Wing February 1966,
Waddington Wing February 1968. Crashed
near Wingate on 8 January 1971 following a
engine bay fire, all crew escaped successfully.
Struck off charge on 11 January 1971.

*Goose Bay January 1969. Whilst being
pushed out of the hangar the port leg fell
through an underfloor heating duct.*

Vulcan B Mk.2 **XM611**

Completed on 12 February 1964 with Olympus 301
engines. **Served with:** IX Squadron February 1964
Coningsby Wing, Waddington Wing May 1968, 101
Squadron May 1972. Transferred to St. Athan on 27 January
1982. Sold to T. Bradbury as scrap on 2 June 1983.

SURVIVOR

Vulcan B Mk.2 **XM612**

Completed on 28 February 1964 with Olympus 301
engines. **Served with:** IX Squadron March 1964
Coningsby Wing July 1966, Cottesmore Wing November
1965. A&AEE March 1968, Waddington Wing April 1968,
101 Squadron May 1975, 44 Squadron July 1981. Modified
for 'Black Buck' operations. 44 Squadron May 1982. Sold
to Norwich Aviation Museum on 19 January 1983 and
delivered on 30 January 1983.

Vulcan B Mk.2 **XM645**

Completed on 10 March 1964 with Olympus 301 engines.
Served with: Coningsby Wing March 1964, Cottesmore
Wing January 1965, Waddington Wing January 1967, 230
OCU August 1968, Waddington Wing April 1967, 101
Squadron August 1973, Akrotiri Wing March 1974, IX
Squadron January 1975. Crashed at Zabbar, Malta on 14
October 1975. Undershot runway at Luqa and blew up
while attempting to climb away, pilots ejected but rear crew
all killed.

XM

Vulcan B Mk.2 **XM646**

Completed on 7 April 1964 with Olympus 301 engines. **Served with:** 12 Squadron April 1964 Coningsby Wing, Cottesmore Wing April 1965, Akrotiri Wing February 1969, IX Squadron January 1975, 101 Squadron June 1981. Moved to St. Athan on 26 January 1982 and sold to T. Bradbury as scrap on 29 June 1983.

Vulcan B Mk.2 **XM647**

Completed on 15 April 1964 with Olympus 301 engines. **Served with:** 35 Squadron Coningsby Wing April 1964, Cottesmore Wing January 1966, Akrotiri Wing February 1969, Waddington Wing January 1975, 44 Squadron September 1979 and 50 Squadron September 1981. Delivered to Laarbruch on 17 September 1982 for ground instruction as No.(8765M). Sold to Solair UK on 25 February 1985 as scrap.

Vulcan B Mk.2 **XM648**

Completed on 5 May 1964 with Olympus 301 engines. **Served with:** IX Squadron May 1964 Coningsby Wing, Cottesmore Wing March 1966, Waddington Wing January 1968, 101 Squadron May 1972, 44 Squadron May 1975, 101 Squadron March 1977, IX Squadron September 1980, 101 Squadron October 1981. Grounded on 10 September 1982. Sold to Bird Group as scrap on 8 December 1982.

Vulcan B Mk.2 **XM649**

Completed on 12 May 1964 with Olympus 301 engines. **Served with:** IX Squadron Coningsby Wing May 1964, Cottesmore Wing June 1965, Waddington Wing January 1968, 101 Squadron August 1973, IX Squadron April 1976, 101 Squadron August 1979. Moved to St. Athan on 2 September 1981 and sold to Bird Group as scrap on 2 December 1982.

Fred Martin

Vulcan B Mk.2 **XM650**

Completed on 27 May 1964 with Olympus 301 engines.
Served with: 12 Squadron Coningsby Wing June
1964, Cottesmore Wing May 1965, Waddington Wing
December 1967, 44 Squadron May 1975. Moved to St.
Athan on 28 January 1982 and allocated No.(8748M) on
16 March 1983. Sold to Bournewood Aviation as scrap on
22 March 1984.

Vulcan B Mk.2 **XM651**

Completed on 19 June 1964 with Olympus 301 engines.
Served with: 12 Squadron Coningsby Wing June 1964,
Cottesmore Wing September 1965, Waddington Wing
April 1968, 101 Squadron May 1972, 50 Squadron
September 1975, 101 Squadron September 1979.
Grounded on 10 September 1982. Sold to Bird Group as
scrap on 30 November 1982.

Vulcan B Mk.2 **XM652**

Completed on 12 August 1964 with Olympus 301
engines. **Served with:** IX Squadron Coningsby Wing
August 1964, Cottesmore Wing July 1965, Waddington
Wing December 1967, 44 Squadron September 1975,
IX Squadron October 1981, 50 Squadron October 1982.
Sold to Boulding Group on 20 February 1984. Dismantled
and transported to Sheffield on 7 May 1984. Nose section
to Burntwood in February 1985. The remaining airframe
scrapped in February 1985.

Vulcan B Mk.2 **XM653**

Completed on 31 August 1964 with Olympus 301 engines.
Served with: IX Squadron Coningsby Wing August
1964, Cottesmore Wing July 1965, Waddington Wing
January 1968, 101 Squadron May 1972, 44 Squadron
May 1975, IX Squadron September 1975, 101 Squadron
October 1978, IX Squadron May 1979 and 101 Squadron
July 1979. Moved to St. Athan on 10 September 1979
for assessment of damage to structure from a hot air leak
whilst inbound at Goose Bay. Classified Cat 5(c) spares
recovery and scrapped on 28 July 1981.

XM

Vulcan B Mk.2 **XM654**

Completed on 22 October 1964 with Olympus 301 engines. **Served with:** 12 Squadron Coningsby Wing October 1964, Cottesmore Wing October 1965, Waddington Wing April 1968, 101 Squadron August 1973, 50 Squadron September 1975, 101 Squadron September 1981 and 50 Squadron October 1981. Aircraft grounded on 29 October 1982 and sold to Bird Group as scrap on 30 November 1982.

Vulcan B Mk.2 **XM655**

Completed on 19 November 1964 with Olympus 301 engines. **Served with:** IX Squadron Cottesmore Wing November 1964, Waddington Wing January 1968, 44 Squadron July 1981 and 50 Squadron August 1982. Sold to Roy Jacobsen on 11 February 1984 and delivered to Wellesbourne Mountford on 11 February 1984. Registered G-VULC on 27 February 1984. Re-registered N655AV in 1985. Sold to Radar Moor in 1992. Maintained in taxiing condition by 655 Maintenance and Preservation Society.

SURVIVOR

Vulcan B Mk.2 **XM656**

Completed on 11 December 1964 with Olympus 301 engines. **Served with:** 35 Squadron Cottesmore Wing December 1964, Waddington Wing February 1968, 101 Squadron September 1975 and IX Squadron December 1980. Moved to Cottesmore for display on 9 August 1982. Allocated No.(8757M) for crash rescue training at RAF Cottesmore. Sold to Bird Group as scrap on 30 March 1983.

Vulcan B Mk.2 **XM657**

Completed on 14 January 1965 with Olympus 301 engines. **Served with:** 35 Squadron Cottesmore Wing January 1965, Waddington Wing March 1968, 101 Squadron May 1972 and 44 Squadron April 1980. Allocated to Central Training Establishment on 5 January 1982 and delivered to Manston on 12 January 1982. Allocated No.(8734M). Later scrapped.
Last production B Mk.2 Vulcan.

Squadron Insignia

Crests and Badges of the Royal Air Force Squadrons in which the Vulcans served - 1955 to 1993

617 Squadron

Motto: *Aprés moi, le déluge - (After me, the flood)*

Badge: *On a roundel, a wall in fesse, fracted by three flashes of lightning in pile and issuant from the breach water proper - approved by King George VI in March 1944. The broken dam is indicative of the successful attack on the Rhur dams in May 1943.*

Formed at Scampton on 21 March 1943 specifically to undertake one operation - Operation Chastise - the breaching of German dams. Equipped with Vulcans at Scampton from May 1958 to December 1981.

230 Operational Conversion Unit

Motto: *Temper the Sword*

Formed at Lindholme by renaming No 1653 Conversion Unit on 15 March 1947. Trained Vulcan crews at Waddington from 1956 until 1961, when it moved to Finningley, before finally moving to Scampton from 1969 to August 1981.

9 (IX) Squadron

Motto: *Per noctem volamus - (Throughout the night we fly)*

Badge: *A bat - approved by King Edward VIII in November 1936 as an authorised version of a badge highlighting the Squadron's night-bombing duties.*

Formed at St Omer, France on 8 December 1914 by renaming the Wireless Flight of the RFC Headquarters. Equipped with the Vulcan B2 in 1962. Moved to Cottesmore in 1964, and Akrotiri in 1969 along with 35 Squadron. Returned to Waddington from 1975 to 1982.

12 (B) Squadron

Motto: *Leads the Field*

Badge: *A fox's mask - approved by King George VI in February 1937. Based on a suggestion when the squadron was equipped with the Fairey Fox, an aircraft of which they were proud and the sole operators.*

Formed on 14 February 1915 at Netheravon from a nucleus of crew and aircraft provided by No. 1 Squadron. Equipped with Vulcans from 1962 to 1967 at Coningsby, and won the 1964 US Strategic Air Command bombing competition.

27 Squadron

Motto: *Quam celerrime ad astra - (With all speed to the Stars)*

Badge: *An elephant - approved by HM King Edward VIII in October 1936. The badge was based on an unofficial emblem first used in 1934 and commemorates the Squadron's first operational aircraft - the Martinsyde G100 'Elephant' - and the unit's long sojourn to India.*

Formed at Hounslow on 5 November 1915 from a nucleus provided by No. 24 Squadron. Equipped with Vulcans at Scampton in April 1961 until 1983.

35 (XXXV) Squadron

Motto: *Uno animo agimus - (We act with one accord)*

Badge: *A horse's head winged. The badge commemorates co-operation with the Calvary during the First World War.*

Formed on 1 February 1916 at Thetford, Norfolk, from a nucleus flight of No.9 (Reserve) Squadron, RFC. Equipped with Vulcans in December 1962 at Coningsby, moving to Cottesmore in November 1964. Joined the Near East Strike Force at Akrotiri from 1969 to 1974 (with IX Squadron) as part of the UK contribution to CENTO the Central Treaty Organisation. Returned to UK at Scampton from 1975 to 1982.

44 (Rhodesia) Squadron

Motto: *Fulmina regis iusta - (The King's thunderbolts are righteous)*

Badge: *On a mount an elephant. Based upon the seal of Lo Bengula, the chief of the Matabeles on conquest. The seal shows an elephant which, in the case of this unit, is intended to indicate heavy attacks.*

Formed at Hainault Farm, Essex, on 24th July 1917, as a Home Defence Squadron. Title altered to 'No. 44 (Rhodesia) Squadron' in September 1941, in recognition of that country's generous donations to the war effort. Equipped with Vulcans at Waddington in August 1960 until December 1982.

50 Squadron

Motto: *Sic fidem servamus - (Thus we keep faith)*

Badge: *A sword in bend severing a mantle palewise. This unit formed at Dover and adopted a mantle being severed by a sword to show its connection with that town, the arms of which include St. Martin and the beggar with whom he divided his cloak. The mantle is also indicative of the protection given to this country by the Royal Air Force. The running dogs device on squadron aircraft arose from the radio call sign Dingo that the squadron was allocated as part of the Home Defence network in 1918.*

Formed at Dover, Kent, on 15 May 1916, as a Home Defence squadron. Equipped with Vulcans at Waddington in August 1961 until March 1984.

83 Squadron

Motto: *Strike to defend*

Badge: *An attire. The red deer's antler is in reference to the squadron's association with Scotland. The attire has six points commemorating an outstanding occasion in the First World War when six DFCs were awarded for one operation. The antler in black affords reference to night flying and the three top points stand for the crown of success met with by the squadron.*

Formed at Montrose, Scotland, on 7 January 1917. Equipped with Vulcans at Waddington in July 1957, then based at Scampton from October 1957 to August 1969.

101 Squadron

Motto: *Mens agitat molem - (Mind over matter)*

Badge: *Issuant from the battlements of a tower, a demi lion rampant guardant - approved by King George VI in February 1938. The battlements symbolise the Squadron's pioneering role in the development of power-operated gun turrets, while the lion indicates the unit's fighting power and spirit.*

Formed at South Farnborough on 12 July 1917. Equipped with Vulcans in October 1957 as part of the Finningley Wing and based at Waddington from 1961 until 1982.

Group and Wing Insignia

1 Group

Motto: *Swift To Attack*

Badge: *A black panther's head erased. The badge commemorates the move of No 1 Group to France as the Advanced Air Striking force in September 1939. It was code-named 'Panther', and the formation was always known by this title.*

Formed on 1 April 1918 as part of the South Eastern Area.

Waddington Wing

In 1957 Waddington became a Vulcan base, hosting the first Vulcan squadron formed, the re-born No. 83, later joined by a re-formed No. 44 Squadron. No. 83 Squadron eventually moved elsewhere but over the next 15 years Waddington gathered three other Vulcan squadrons. Vulcans of the Wing carried the City of Lincoln shield on their tailfins.

Finningley Wing

Finningley re-opened as a V-bomber station in 1957 after two years work re-laying and extending the main runway and building Unit stores for atomic weapons. No. 101 Squadron operated Vulcans there until 1961 when it changed places with No. 230 Operational Conversion Unit, which remained at Finningley with Vulcans until 1968. Aircraft carried the Yorkshire Rose on their tailfins.

Display Team Insignia

As display aircraft XL426 and XH558 wore the Panther's head of 1 Group

Popular Culture

Public interest in the Vulcan was high from the start, in no small part due to its futuristic design, unlike any other aircraft of the period. Its sleek, minimalist appearance captured the imagination and was in stark contrast to the propeller driven aircraft that had been at the cutting edge only a few years previously. This interest was reflected in the media and elsewhere, with newspaper and magazine features, advertising (Avro being keen to show off their new baby), children's books, comics, and toys.

Comics and books

In the 1960s and 70s, interest in the V-Bombers was reflected in three children's comics, named after the trio. The Victor was published weekly by D.C. Thomson, running for a massive 1,657 issues from 1961 right through to 1992. It featured adventure tales in the 'Boy's Own' style, many set in the two World Wars. Valiant, a boys adventure comics anthology, and one of publisher IPC's major adventure titles, ran from 1962 to 1976. Its popularity was marked in 2012 when it was included in a Royal Mail stamp collection celebrating Britain's rich comic book history, alongside the likes of The Beano, The Dandy and Eagle. Vulcan was short-lived, running for just 28 issues from 1975 until 1976, reprinting material from Lion and Valiant.

The Avro Vulcan design inspired many comic and children's book publishers to run features on it. L. Ashwell Wood produced a beautiful colour cutaway for Eagle comic in 1958, and T. E. North used the Vulcan for his frontispiece painting in Collins' 'Timothy's Book of Aircraft' (part of their 'Wonder Books' series). Ladybird's The Story of Flight showed a Vulcan being escorted by three Lightning interceptors, and their 'The Airman in the Royal Air Force' featured the aircraft extensively, with three paintings of the Vulcan and a further one of its Blue Steel

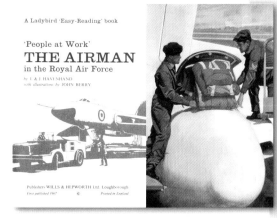

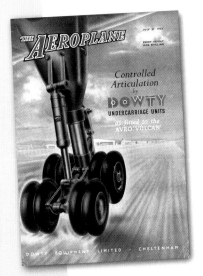

Top: The V-Bomber comics Vulcan, Victor and Valiant. Above: The cover and an inside page of Airman in the Royal Air Force from the Ladybird 'People at Work' series, 1967, illustrated by John Berry.

Left: A Dowty advert on the cover of Aeroplane, July 1953, and The Lion Book of Speed cover by James McConnell, 1962.

The Thunderball mock-up under constuction in the Bahamas. *William Creighton* The scale model at Bruntingthorpe in 2009 as the crew celebrate the successful conclusion of a fundraising campaign. *Les Wilson*

Below: Commando from 2005 illustrated by Ian Kennedy, and a 1980 copy of The Penetrators, cover by Brian Knight.

weapon. Other examples include the Lion Book of Speed in 1962 and, more recently, a 2005 issue of war comic Commando.

In the 1965 Cold War novel 'The Penetrators' by Hank Searls (writing as Anthony Gray), an RAF officer leads nine Vulcans in a maverick mock attack against the USA in order to prove that the manned bomber is a more flexible deterrent option than ballistic missiles. Published in 2006, the best-selling 'Vulcan 607' by Rowland White tells the dramatic story of the first Black Buck mission, and Vulcans are the central feature of the novel 'Hullo Russia, Goodbye England' (2009) by Derek Robinson, where a WWII Lancaster pilot rejoins the RAF at the height of the Cold War.

TV and Film
In 1953, the Shell Film Unit produced a short film on the Vulcan, directed by Peter De Normanville, and the little-known 1958 Italian sci-fi film 'La Morte Viene Dallo Spazio' (The Day The Sky Exploded) uses a clip of a white flash Vulcan at low level. The 1960 made for cinemas colour documentary 'Delta 8-3' examined life at RAF Waddington, watching the training of a new Vulcan crew, but the aircraft's most notable role came in the James Bond movie 'Thunderball' (1965). Agents of SPECTRE hijack a Vulcan B.1a bomber to use its two NATO nuclear bombs for a ransom plot. In Ian Fleming's original novel, the bomber is known as the (fictional) Villiers Vindicator. Two aircraft from the Waddington Wing were used in filming, XA913 for ground sequences and XH506 for in flight shots. A large scale model used in the film used to reside with XH558 at Bruntingthorpe. For underwater location shooting in the Bahamas, a full-size mock-up was constructed of the forward section and underside, including landing gear, and the remains are still a popular diving attraction. In Ridley Scott's 1979 film 'Alien', parts from scrapped Vulcans were used to make the set of the spaceship Nostromo.

Appearances in TV shows include 'The Master Minds' episode of The Avengers (1965) in which all three V-bombers feature, and a Blue Steel equipped Vulcan can be seen in The Champions series ('The

Opposite page, left to right: Avro advert, Meccano Magazine cover for March 1953, Ladybird's The Story of Flight (1960) and Look and Learn (1961), depicting the engine failure suffered by XM610 in 1971, by artist Wilf Hardy. Note the three trailing static lines indicating the rear crew have parachuted out.

Right: A dramatic scene from the Mach1 strip in 2000AD, illustrated by Ian Kennedy.

Silent Enemy', 1969). In the 1995 series Bugs, a car crashes into XL426 in the episode 'All Under Control' (actually hitting a lorry trailer in front of the aircraft, thankfully!). A nod to the Vulcan can be found in the sci-fi comedy 'Hyperdrive' (2006-7), where the spaceship HMS Camden Lock carries the serial XH558.

As the fleet was being retired in the 1980s, Central Television filmed 'The Last Days of a Vulcan Squadron' in 1982, looking at the history of 617 Squadron, and following one of the aircrews on their last sortie. More recently, journalist and presenter John Sergeant flew alongside XH558 for a feature in the BBC's 'Britain's Hidden Heritage' programme, and Channel 4 produced a documentary about the first Black Buck mission, 'The Falkland's Most Daring Raid.'

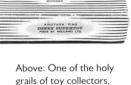

Above: One of the holy grails of toy collectors, the very rare Dinky Vulcan from 1955-56.

Above: Corgi's commemorative limited edition model of XM597 from 2002.

Toys and models

In the mid 1950s, Dinky produced a simple diecast toy of the Vulcan B1. At over 6 inches wide it would have been heavy to cast in the usual zinc alloy Mazak, and there was a shortage of the material due to the Korean War, so aluminium was used instead. Sold only in Canada, the model suffered from casting problems and only around 500 were made before the high temperatures of aluminium casting meant the mould became unusable, making it a rare and very collectable toy. White metal and resin replicas have since been produced. Corgi continue to make limited edition 1/144 scale diecast collectors models of various Vulcan airframes, including three versions of XH558, and smaller 'fit the box' models of XH558 and XL426.

Below: Polish magazine Latajace Fortece issue 6 from 2011.

Below: The current version of the Airfix 1/72 Vulcan kit and the same kit issued under license by MPC in the United States.

Del Prado manufactured a 1/234 scale diecast, branding the model as XM571, and Model Power issued the same in the USA (in their Postage Stamp Planes range), painted as XH558 (somewhat inaccurately as the model had 300 series jet nozzles). Richmond Models made a Vulcan to the Sky branded toy of XH558 in 2009 and, in 2011, Polish magazine 'Latajace Fortece' (Flying Fortresses) issued a 1/144 version diecast of XH558 as a cover mount. Recently Dragon Wings and Gemini Jets started to issue 1/200 scale diecasts and kits, and a number of manufacturers have produced large scale models carved in wood.

The Vulcan has been well (if not always accurately) represented in kit form, with the Airfix 1/72 scale model still in production having being reissued several times since its debut in the late 1970s. The kit is currently marketed as XH558, although it represents an airframe with 300 series engine nozzles. The same kit is sold under the MPC brand in the United States. Airfix weren't the first though, Frog made a B1 in 1958 at 1/96 scale, and many other kits have been issued in a variety of scales over the years, by Lindbergh/Revell (1/96 with straight leading edge), Rareplane (vacform 1/72 kit), Welsh Models (1/144) and Aeroclub (vacform, resin and white metal 1/48).

A selection of Vulcan stamps and first day covers, including the Royal Mail air displays set, issued in 2008 to commemorate the first powered flight in the UK at Farnborough in 1908.

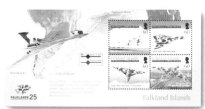

Stamps and ephemera

Bletchley Park have issued several stamp sets linked to the Vulcan (and XH558 in particular). Not surprisingly, the Vulcan is a popular feature of Falkland Island stamps and, in the 1980s, there were several first day covers issued to mark the disbandment of Vulcan squadrons and to commemorate the Falklands. Anniversaries also provided opportunities to celebrate the type, with the 50th Anniversary of the Vulcan, and 80th Anniversary of the RAF.

Cigarette cards originated in America in the 1880s and quickly made their way to the UK, where W.D. & H.O. Wills popularised them, with thousands of sets being issued by hundreds of manufacturers in the early 1900s. Needless to say, the Vulcan appeared on various sets, and as the production of such cards diminished the aircraft made its way onto phonecards, including a BT card marking XH558s last flight in 1993. Playing cards have also carried the Vulcan image, with Avro itself producing a complimentary set in the late 1950s.

Now of course, with the successful return to flight, media coverage has increased notably, with regular magazine features and XH558's own official Facebook page and Twitter feed. Merchandise plays an important part in the ongoing funding of the last airworthy Vulcan, and a new generation is being introduced to the aircraft through calendars, jigsaws, posters, DVDs and books like this one!

BT phonecard from 1993 in commemoration of XH558s last flight.

Above: 1950s Vulcan playing card pack by John Waddington & Co.

Right: Vulcan cigarette cards by Wills's Castella Cigars (1994), Turf Cigarettes (1953) and Topps Jets (USA, 1956).

Epilogue

On 4 January 1967, land and water speed record-breaker Donald Campbell lost his life attempting to raise the world water speed record above 300mph. His first run on Coniston Water in his Bluebird K7 hydroplane achieved an average of 297.6mph, but on the return run at over 300mph the boat lifted from the water surface, somersaulted in mid-air and crashed back into the lake.

The day after the accident a lone Vulcan reportedly flew over the lake, dipping its wings in tribute, though the RAF denied it at the time, and the story passed into Bluebird legend.

Behind the scenes though, things got a little hot for the pilot, Don Dale, who had been grounded on landing and was about to be grilled by the AOC for his spontaneous tribute. In 2004, he was contacted via the Key Publishing forum and recalled:

"The Vulcan in question was XM657, Cottesmore Wing, 12(B) Squadron Crew. Briefed for 2 Low Levels, entering in the West Country. Gin clear day. We could see Hilpsford Point (Barrow) coasting out of North Wales. Radar and plotting gear was switched off. Began a climb to 2000'. Nav plotter went to the bomb aimers window for back up map reading.

"We flew over Coniston and dipped our wings in tribute to a very brave man who had just lost his life. We re-entered the Low Level route at the next radar significant point and completed a successful RBS delivery on West Freugh, then back to the West Country for another Low Level run along the same route. This time, there was no deviation and we returned to base. Then it became exciting...

"It had been on the radio at lunchtime, it was in all the evening newspapers, and headlines in the National Press the next morning, quote "Bomber Command, on being approached, said it was not one of ours".

"Poignantly, on recovery of Bluebird and of Donald Campbell, his internment ceremony was planned to have a flypast of 4 Tornados, sadly, the weather was too bad for the flypast. Perhaps I was 25 years too early, but I had given him an appropriate salute. I was not off track and I was 2000' feet over the surface of the lake, so not illegally low flying off the Low Level route but flying safely and with due consideration to normal decent convention to the family and to the deceased.

"Had I asked for formal permission, I guess it would have took months to get a negative answer. They finally got me for leaving the Low Level route when not authorised to do so. When I asked for clarification of this, I recall that I received the "GET OUT" response!!"

RIP Donald...

XH558 in the Lake District in 2011. *Tom Hill*

XH558 and Spitfire, Sywell 2012.
Charles Toop

Opposite: The first, VX770 in
1952 and the last, XH558 in
2012. *Cyril Peckham and Laurens
van de Craats*

The authors and publisher would like to acknowledge and thank the following individuals and sources:

Robert Miller and John Wood for airframes research, Craig Bulman for researching XH558's service history and associated photos; RAF/MoD; Kev Darling - *Avro Vulcan* (Crowood Press); Robert Jackson - *Avro Vulcan* (Patrick Stephens Ltd); Tony Blackman - *Vulcan Test Pilot* (Grub Street); Philip Birtles - *The Avro Vulcan* (Ian Allen); Craig Bulman - *The Vulcan B.Mk2 From a Different Angle* (Pentland Books); Duncan Cubitt & Ken Ellis - *Vulcan, Last of the V-Bombers* (Chancellor Press); David W. Fildes - *The Avro Type 698 Vulcan* (Pen & Sword Aviation); Tim Laming - *The Vulcan Story* (W&N); Haynes - *Avro Vulcan Workshop Manual*; A.D. George - *A Note on A.V. Roe and the Brownsfield Mill, Ancoats*; Air Britain: *RAF Aircraft XA100 - XZ999* ; The Vulcan Magazine; Meccano Magazine; A.V. Roe Family Website; Avro Heritage Website; www.vulcantothesky.org; National Archives, Kew; Key Publishing; Professional Pilots Rumour Network; Daily Telegraph; Daily Mirror; Mail on Sunday; Getty Images; Charles Toop; Terry Senior, Andrew Brown, Frank Grealish, Laurens van de Craats; bearalley.blogspot.co.uk; thunder-and-lightnings.co.uk; Andy Leitch - *Vulcans in Camera*, avrovulcan.org.uk; Fred Martin at RZF Digital Imaging.